GROWTH & CONTRACTION
SCOTTISH INDUSTRY c.1860–1990

PETER L. PAYNE

The Economic &
Social History
Society of Scotland

1992

© 1992 The Economic and Social History Society of Scotland

ISBN: 0 9516044 1 4

Cover Design by Stevenson Graphics

Typeset & Printed by Stevenson (Printers) Ltd., Dundee ☎ (0382) 25768

ACKNOWLEDGEMENTS

I would like to thank the General Editor of the series, Professor R.H. Campbell, for help in the preparation of this study; all those who have permitted me to quote from their unpublished theses; Mr J.B.K. Hunter for information on some aspects of the history of J. & P. Coats; and Mrs Norma Sim for typing and retyping drafts of steadily diminishing length.

CONTENTS

INTRODUCTION

In July 1991, the Chairman of British Steel, Sir Robert Scholey, told Scottish shareholders, bitterly critical of the company's refusal to refurbish its Dalzell Works, 'You are looking backwards all the time. Look to the future. Don't look to the past'. What Lanarkshire needed, he said, was 'new employment based on new jobs with new technology'. (*Times*, 1 August 1991). Objectively, British Steel's decision is incontrovertible and its chairman's prescription for Scotland's future economic wellbeing, incontestable. In the last three decades the sinews of the traditional Scottish economy have withered away, leaving an industrial sector apparently without internal dynamism, bereft of heroic entrepreneurs, and peculiarly vulnerable to what sometimes appears to be the irrational dictates of managers located far beyond its borders. In retrospect, the demise of so much of Scotland's industry has the inevitability of a Greek tragedy. This brief essay will chronicle and attempt to explain the rise and painful contraction of Scotland's labour-intensive staple industries.

I

Precarious Prosperity
c.1860–1913

Textiles

Textiles are not synonymous with cotton; nor was the decline of cotton synchronous with its disappearance. In 1857 the embroidered muslin trade abruptly collapsed, bringing down a number of major firms in Glasgow. No sooner had this disaster been overcome than the entire industry was confronted by the disruption of cotton supplies during the American Civil War. And if this 'did not cause the end of the days of prosperity of the Scottish cotton industry' (Campbell, 1965, 110), it can hardly have failed to dissuade potential new entrants to the industry. For all that, by 1868 Bremner was able to assert, without apparent irony, that 'the cotton manufacture has now nearly resumed its normal condition' (Bremner, 1868, 288). There were still 131 cotton mills operating in Scotland when he wrote, compared with 163 on the eve of the Civil War, and Robertson has detected 'signs that [the cotton industry] was perhaps healthier in 1867 than in 1861' (Robertson, 1970, 120). If so, it was a final flourish. As overseas competitors, assisted by tariffs, captured their own domestic markets and responded to competitive forces by moving into fine cottons, Scottish 'fancies' came under increasing pressure, not least from Lancashire. Continued survival became dependent upon enhanced labour productivity, itself partially a function of greater capital investment.

In the event, the required response was not forthcoming. In spinning, the low-paid, largely female labour force steadfastly resisted the inducements implicit in piece rates, and weavers refused to contemplate any alteration of the two-loom system which had governed their working lives since the 1830s. With some exceptions, capital investment in the majority of spinning and weaving firms slowed or ceased altogether. This was partly because available funds could more profitably be placed elsewhere – in the heavy industries, shale oil or chemicals, for example – or because the founding families in cotton lost interest in the source of their wealth. There are few more destructive combinations in manufacturing than a recalcitrant labour force and an unmotivated management. Coupled with yet another adverse swing in the cycle of fashion against fine high quality Scottish muslins at the turn of the century, the decline of the Scottish cotton industry after 1870 is readily explicable. By 1910 there were but nine spinning firms left (N.J. Morgan, *DSBB*, I, 297).

It need not have happened, of course. Given more enterprise, the speed of the downturn could have been reduced. That much was demonstrated by the Clyde Spinning Company, established in 1871 and equipped with the most modern machinery, and by the Glasgow Cotton Spinning Company, founded in 1883 and modelled on the Oldham limited companies. It was said that the latter company was 'the only concern [in Scotland] which meets the Lancashire establishments on their own ground, and . . . its experience proves that commercial success is possible with capital, experience, and the right methods' (Robertson, 1970, 126; and see N.J. Morgan, *DSBB*, I, 383–4, 396).

Another firm with 'the right methods' was J. & P. Coats who by 1914 were to dominate the world market in sewing thread (Cairncross and Hunter, 1987; Hunter, *DSBB*, I, 329–34). Concentrating on the production of sixcord cotton thread, the firm was admirably placed to exploit the vast and growing market created by the rapid spread of the sewing machine in the 1850s. Despite the doubling and redoubling of the capacity of the mills at Ferguslie, the American market, which was already absorbing over 80 per cent of sales, was insatiable. This created opportunities for others. They were seized by domestic manufacturers and by Coats' arch rivals, J. & J. Clark (N.J. Morgan, *DSBB*, I, 326–28). By the 1870s, the absorption of competitors, the establishment of mills overseas and massive investment had given Clarks the leadership of the British home market, Coats had become dominant in America, and the two firms fought out supremacy with other British firms elsewhere in the thread-using world.

This state of affairs brought increasing dissatisfaction to Archibald Coats. In 1878 he created the pivotal post of foreign sales manager and appointed Otto Ernst Philippi from the firm's Hamburg agency to it. Within a decade, Philippi had completely reorganised and rationalised Coats' marketing arrangements in Europe and the non-English-speaking world (J.B.K. Hunter, *DSBB*, I, 389–92). From possessing a destabilising degree of autonomy, the distributors of Coats' thread were brought under central control and formal and informal agreements about prices and market shares had been made with the firm's major competitors, including Clarks.

The logical consequences of these developments was the integration of the production and ownership of the associated firms. It came in 1896 by a merger which amalgamated Coats, Clarks, Jonas Brook of Meltham, Yorkshire, and another major British firm, James Chadwick of Eagley Mills, Bolton. Having an original capital of nearly £8m., J. & P. Coats Ltd. was to be perhaps the most efficient of all the British nineteenth century combinations. By 1913, in addition to Britain, the United States and Canada, Coats were manufacturing in ten countries in Europe and in Brazil, Mexico and Japan. The group comprised some 40 associated and subsidiary concerns, but this was no loose combination like so many large British companies of the time. Detailed control was exercised from

Glasgow. Even the growing army of shareholders was kept at arm's length. They, averred a writer in *The Investors' Review*, were regarded by the Coats family as 'necessary inconveniences, to be as much as possible ignored' (*Investors' Review*, Vol. VI, November 1895). And yet even this critic was forced to conclude that 'J. & P. Coats . . . continues to flourish'. It was to do so far into the next century (N.J. Morgan and J.B.K. Hunter, *DSBB*, I; Cairncross and Hunter, 1987; Macrosty, 1907; Payne, 1967a).

The same cannot be said of some of the other branches of the cotton industry in Scotland. By the third quarter of the nineteenth century the bleaching, printing and dyeing trades contained some of the largest and most prosperous companies in the textiles sector. 'The jewel in the crown' was the Thornliebank print works, founded in 1780. Under Walter Crum it became 'the largest and best equipped works in the world' (Turnbull, 1951, 93), and under his eldest son, Alexander, a policy of aggressive expansion coupled with continuous re-equipment and diversification culminated in the flotation of the Thornliebank Company Ltd. in 1886, with a nominal capital of £250,000. By this time the firm had moved into the production of Holland cloth and Turkey-red dyeing, a specialised trade that had undergone massive expansion in the Vale of Leven during the 1870s. This step proved fatal. Weakened by excess production, Thornliebank's profitability became dangerously erratic. When Alexander Crum died in 1893, his desperate successors swept the firm into the ill-conceived Calico Printers' Association and the subsequent history of Thornliebank 'was to be one of decline and gradual closure in favour of its less distinguished English counterparts' (N.J. Morgan, *DSBB*, I, 384; for the general context, see Payne, 1967a, 528–9; Turnbull, 1951, Appendix 6, 436–58; Cook, 133–211).

A major reason why Thornliebank joined the Calico Printers' Association was the decision taken one year earlier by the dyers in the Vale of Leven to form the United Turkey Red Company Ltd. This combine escaped many of the difficulties experienced by the CPA. Only a few firms were involved and overall direction of the United Turkey Red Company came to reside in the hands of one man, John H. Christie, managing partner of John Orr Ewing & Company, since 1878 the dominant firm in the industry in Scotland. Christie was that great rarity in nineteenth century British business, a fully trained and qualified chemist with a passion for systematic research into the mysteries of textile dyeing and colouring. Under his chairmanship (N.J. Morgan, *DSBB*, I, 320–21) there was every reason to expect that the United Turkey Red Company would overcome the difficulties that had brought about its creation and sustain this branch of Scotland's textile industry in the future.

In the east of Scotland, the linen trade – encompassing the manufacture of heavy linens, hemp and jute – had become predominant. Flax spinning contracted severely during the second half of the nineteenth century, its home and overseas markets eroded by foreign competition. Firms continued to prosper if, like J. & G. Paton of Montrose, they moved up market and adapted their productive capacity to the finest quality yarn, or if they integrated forward into weaving and finishing, which provided more scope for the adoption of new cost-reducing technology and more efficient internal organisation. Of the latter group, Baxter Brothers of Dundee was by far the largest and most successful, but by the time that Peter Carmichael, to whom much of this success may be attributed, had become senior partner in 1872, the great days were over and Baxters had lost their momentum (E. Gauldie, *DSBB*, I, 318; Lenman *et al.*, 1969, 46–8).

During the 1850s the *domestic* market for home-produced linens experienced the initial, rapid stage of its secular decline, shrinking to perhaps half its former size in less than a decade. Inferior to cotton in design, colour and finish and, above all, rendered more expensive by its dependence on an increasingly deficient supply of flax, linen could not hope to retain its former importance (Rimmer, 1960, 228–31). Some firms in the industry sought salvation in specialisation either upon finer linens, bleached goods, diapers and damasks, as in north Fife, or on heavy linens like osnaburgs, sheeting and dowlais, in the production of which Forfar and Brechin became prominent. But most of the great Dundee firms moved into jute. Those who got in first, like the Cox Brothers and Gilroy & Company gained a head start which they never lost (Howe, 1982, 9–10; Lenman *et al.*, 1969, 24).

Cox Brothers were to dominate the industry until 1920. At their integrated works, using raw jute packed by their Indian subsidiary, Cox Brothers produced a remarkable range of products, including sacking, bagging, tarpaulins, twines, cords, ropes, woolpacks for the colonies and matting. Such diversification, coupled with the world-wide spread of markets and the huge accumulated wealth of the partners, permitted Cox Brothers to withstand the stresses created by a wildly fluctuating demand, rising continental tariffs and ever-increasing competition from Bengal.

Cox Brothers made prodigious profits during the American Civil War and were to do so again during the Franco-Prussian War. Thereafter, the period of 'wonderful prosperity' came to an end. Many firms went out of business and there seems to have been little technical innovation in the industry (Lenman *et al.*, 1969, 54). There was still money to be made in the trade, but the opportunities for doing so were fitful and all too often dependent on government contracts or on spasmodic attempts to squeeze greater gross returns from a large production of materials yielding only miniscule unit profit margins, a tactic employed disastrously by Andrew Lowson & Company of Arbroath.

By 1914 the outlook was decidedly unhealthy (Lenman *et al.*, 1969, 35–7). There was only one area of expansion: linoleum. In 1838 Michael Nairn, the proprietor of a large canvas factory in Kirkcaldy, had introduced the manufacture of floorcloth canvas and by 1876, 'having revolutionalised the production of floorcloth', Nairn began to make linoleum (N.J. Morgan,

DSBB, I, 1986, 381; Muir, 1956, 19–37). The new product enjoyed a vigorous domestic and overseas demand and when the firm's exports were threatened by rising tariffs, subsidiary manufacturing companies were established in the United States (1886), France (1898) and Germany (c.1900). In Kirkcaldy, meanwhile, there was no waning in technical progressiveness. Spurred on by fierce competition from other local firms, several of which owed their genesis to Michael Nairn's ex-partners or managerial staff, Nairns introduced the manufacture of cork-carpet, the mechanisation of linoleum and floorcloth printing, and the development of a form of inlaid linoleum. By the turn of the century, Nairn's major rivals were Barry, Ostlere & Shepherd Ltd., and Shepherd & Beveridge (N.J. Morgan, *DSBB*, I, 307–309). With these three firms battling for the leadership of the industry, themselves harried by several smaller, equally progressive companies, the manufacture of linoleum, backed as it was by woven jute, promised to be a major component of the Dundee trades well into the new century.

If the increasing real wages of the lower middle and working classes during the last quarter of the nineteenth century had served to widen and deepen the domestic market for the products of Kirkcaldy, their social superiors were increasingly able to furnish their homes with rugs and carpeting. Foremost among Scottish firms in this branch of the textile industry was Templetons, whose early growth was based upon the successful exploitation of the Chenille process, patented by James Templeton in 1839. Not until the 1870s did the expansion of the firm falter and profits turn to losses. Attempts to reverse this trend by mechanising the weaving of chenille carpeting were unsuccessful until 1882, when William Adam, a former employee who had established his own business with Michael Tomkinson in Kidderminster, patented a power loom specifically for this purpose. Templetons and two other firms secured a licence to use the new loom, and the four firms, joining together to form the Association of Axminster Manufacturers, agreed to fix prices at a remunerative level (J.N. Bartlett, *DSBB*, I, 406; Bartlett, 1978, 40).

Meanwhile Tomkinson & Adam created an additional market by the use of a power loom of American design which produced carpeting closely resembling but greatly cheaper than hand-tufted Axminster. Only five British firms were licensed to use the loom and in 1878 they too created their own trade association. Within a few years spool Axminster carpeting had built up a significant trade. Templeton broke into this market in 1887 and successfully pressed on his fellow members of the Royal Axminster Manufacturers' Association the necessity of stimulating demand for this product by reducing prices. These tactics saw off a potential American invasion, enhanced the size of the market and by permitting longer runs, greatly reduced oncost charges (Young, 1944, 52–3).

By offering a complete range of carpets, priced to reflect quality differentials and aimed at different segments of the market, Templetons total yardage sales increased and profits rose. On the eve of the First World War Templetons was the largest carpet manufacturer in the United Kingdom, accounting for some 17 per cent of the total output of the industry (J.N. Bartlett, *DSBB*, I, 1986, 407; Young, 1944, 57).

Several ex-employees of Templetons started as independent carpet makers, among them Macfarlane Brothers (1845), John Lyle & Sons (1853) and Anderson & Lawson (1860) originated in this way. There were others in Aberdeen, Edinburgh, Kilmarnock, Paisley and Stirling (Bartlett, 1978, 6). Most were small and short-lived. Scottish firms were particularly important in the manufacture of Tapestry carpets aimed at the lower end of the market, but by the 1890s the firms in this branch of the industry had become victims of an adverse swing in fashion away from their cheap, multi-coloured, picturesque products (Bartlett, 1978, 83; Stoddard, 1962, contains some fine illustrations). Modest profits continued to be made and the major firms at least survived. Others were not so fortunate. In the difficult trading conditions of the opening years of the twentieth century, two of Scotland's oldest carpet makers disappeared: Gregory, Thomson & Co. of Kilmarnock, manufacturers of Brussels carpets, closed down in 1903, and Alexander Hadden & Sons of Aberdeen, a major producer of Kidderminster carpeting a year later (Bartlett, 1978, 14, 78, 79).

If the vagaries of fashion swung against some firms in carpeting, a large number of Scottish concerns in woollen textiles were able to exploit its capriciousness. In cotton, where fashion percolated downwards, boosting the demand as the lower orders aped their betters, in Scottish woollens the reverse occurred. 'From its preoccupation with coarse inferior homespuns for local country wear and fisherfolk Scottish woollen manufacturing after 1830 evolved into the most aristocratic branch of the British wool-textile industry' (Gulvin, 1973, 71, 78). Initial minor variations in the shepherd-check pattern became a flood of 'district checks' and 'clan tartans'.

Although the designs of many of the tartans were spurious, by the 'skilful use of colour, employment of pure virgin wool, and uniqueness of texture . . . The Scottish tweed industry . . . became synonymous with quality' (*Ibid.*, 75, 77). This involved a high degree of specialisation, a policy which was encouraged by the merchants and the high class tailors who by subtle changes in cut, styling and colour sought constantly to maintain the exclusiveness that commended itself to their leisured clientele. Thus, 'Crombie's of Aberdeen became renowned for overcoatings, Roberts' of Selkirk for the higher grade tweeds, Wilson's of Bannockburn for military tartan cloths, [and] Johnston's of Elgin for high quality cashmeres, vicunas and alpacas' (*Ibid.*, 81).

The long term price of these tactics was that the size of the firm remained small; the nature of each company's output often orientated towards the precise requirements of a single merchant. As there were no insurmountable barriers of entry to the industry, the number of mills increased and the size of the workforce rose. Much of this expansion took place in the Borders, especially in Hawick and Galashiels, in the Hillfoots on the northern side of the upper Forth centred on Alloa, and in the north-east of Scotland, where scattered development took place in and around Aberdeen.

This buoyancy was not to continue. The closing decades of the nineteenth century witnessed falling prices, waning demand and the closure of many smaller mills. It was difficult to overcome the adverse effects of rising continental and American tariff barriers. To these difficulties were added fierce overseas competition as Dutch, French and German manufacturers sought, with varying degrees of success, to imitate the products of the Scottish fancy woollen industry and to sell them at lower prices in markets created by British merchants. Cheap French and German products even began to invade the home market, but here the greatest competition stemmed mainly from Yorkshire, whose woollen manufacturers were themselves forced to look for compensation in the domestic market as hostile tariffs also disrupted their international trade. Finally, the pendulum of fashion now swung against 'Scotch tweeds' towards light, less durable smooth-faced fabrics at the very time when the bespoke tailor, the principal outlet for high quality Scottish woollen cloth, began his retreat before the onslaught of the multiple clothier and the ready-made trade.

In these circumstances, only dynamic leadership could avert rapid decline. In many cases, this was lacking. Gulvin has shown that a spirit of inertia and complacency pervaded the industry in the closing years of the nineteenth century. Some firms which 'merely waited for something to turn up', were doomed to extinction. Others, more energetic but misguided, attempted to enlarge sales by moving down market. Costs and hence selling prices were reduced by the use of poor and mixed yarns. These tactics brought only failure to those who adopted them. But there were some who retained their entrepreneurial flair. Several firms invested in new plant, retained their insistence on high quality, and embarked on the production of worsted fabrics that conformed more closely to the general trend in fashion than was possible with woollen tweeds. Others began to explore the burgeoning markets created by the boom in sporting and leisure activities which demanded flannel suiting, or moved into the production of infant shawls; while a few spinners moved into the production of worsted yarns.

One of those who did so, Patons of Alloa, was rewarded by continued expansion, not least because the product of their new combing plant was able to satisfy the sustained demand for yarns for hand-knitting, a pastime which the firm actively encouraged by the publication of a series of guides and handbooks (N.J. Morgan, *DSBB*, I, 388). Another firm, Fleming, Reid & Company took a different and remarkably adventurous route to continued prosperity, creating the chain of 'Scotch Hosiery Stores' through which to sell the firm's products. (C. Munn, *DSBB*, I, 362). The only strategy that even the most far-sighted of the surviving firms refused to contemplate was co-operation with their fellow manufacturers, and merger

– which was the reluctant solution adopted in so many other industries – was anathema to them.

If a major factor in Britain's relative economic decline was the atomistic, competitive organisation of so many of her industries (Elbaun and Lazonick, 1986, 3), the long term prospects for the Scottish fancy woollen industry on the eve of the First World War can only be described as unpromising. But however convincing Lazonick's argument may be when applied to the British cotton industry – the analysis of which inspired his findings – it is patently less so in explaining the fortunes of those manufacturing activities that ultimately depend for their success upon the accurate perception of trends in fashion. Here, relatively small units *may* possess advantages in flexibility and rapidity in response sufficient to compensate for their technological conservatism and high unit costs, and the handful of firms that correctly anticipate consumer demand or build up a loyal clientele will both survive and, occasionally, make handsome profits.

Thus it was with the Border knitwear firms. Emerging in mid-century from a largely 'domestic' hosiery industry producing high quality woollen stockings, numerous firms embarked on the manufacture of woollen underwear, 'much of it of the highest standard of raw materials and finish'. Within a few decades, many 'Scottish hosiery firms had become multi-product businesses manufacturing a bewildering variety of styles, sizes and classes of garment' (Gulvin, 1984, 65, 67), and by 1900, this range of goods was expanded still further by the addition of outerwear: jerseys, sweaters, shawls, cardigans, coats and mufflers.

To secure and retain his individual niche in the market, each manufacturer sought to differentiate his products from his competitors by the use of brand names and by endowing them with some special qualities or distinctive characteristics. By such means many firms survived into the twentieth century. There was little or no recourse to the limited company form: Innes & Henderson (later to be better known as the Braemar Knitwear Ltd.), Peter Scott & Company, Lyle & Scott, all began as partnerships and grew by the retention of profits within their various enterprises, just as Robert Pringle & Son had done since the firm's establishment in 1815. The industry attracted new entrants in other parts of Scotland between 1900 and 1913 and showed a remarkable ability to withstand intense and possibly 'unfair' competition in the home market from German manufacturers, who were accused of dumping goods in the lower quality ranges. Admittedly, an increasing proportion of exports were being sold in Canada, Australia and South Africa, not so much as a drive in 'soft' Empire markets, but because of the impossibility of surmounting the protective walls erected round the American market by the Dingley tariff, estimated to have added perhaps 100 per cent to the prices of garments made in the Borders. Retrospective criticism of the late Victorian British industrialists tends to pay less attention to the malign influence of foreign tariffs than the subject deserves. Be that as it may, in the opening years of the twentieth century this relatively small and localised branch of the textile economy possessed a rare vigour and sensitivity to market opportunity.

Coal

During the period 1831–1911 Scotland's coal industry consistently recorded decennial increases in production above the national average. From an output of almost 3 million tons in 1830, Scottish coal production rose to 8 million tons in the early 1850s, a figure which had doubled by the early 1870s and redoubled by the end of the century, reaching a peak of 42,500,000 tons in 1913 (Church, 1989, 10–11, 25–7).

Explanations of the rise in output emphasise the role of the transport improvement in opening up the Scottish coalfields (Brown, 1953, 6) and the adoption of Neilson's hot blast (A. Slaven, *DSBB*, I, 9). Scotland's proportion of British iron output rose from 5–6 per cent in 1830 to 25–6 per cent in 1860 (Campbell, 1956–7, 283, 285, 287), and every ton of iron produced in Scotland in the middle of the nineteenth century required for its conversion the consumption of about 3.25 tons of coal (Miller, 1864). In the mid-fifties about a third of Scotland's coal output was destined for the furnaces, but by 1870, the proportion had declined to something less than a quarter and by 1885 it was below a tenth (Brown, 1953, 36). The explanation of the continued growth in Scottish coal production between 1855 and 1913, must be sought elsewhere. Exports played a dynamic role, especially after 1880. In addition, by 1913 nearly three million tons of Scottish coal were being shipped coastwise, much of it to London. A similar amount was held in bunkers, a tonnage greater than that being consumed in the manufacture of pig iron (Slaven, 1967, 237; Brown, 1953, 260; Church, 1986, 21–2, 35). The Scottish coal industry also found expanding markets at home for industrial and domestic uses and for the creation and operation of the national railway network. The combined effect of these factors maintained Scotland's share of between 13 to 15 per cent of the coal output of the United Kingdom.

A more sympathetic appreciation of the entrepreneurial behaviour of the Scottish coal masters has recently been emerging. Without denying that as a group 'they were hard-headed businessmen who systematically exploited leases, resources and men, in an era little affected by regulation of hours, wages or safety' (A. Slaven, *DSBB*, I, 10), it would appear that the majority of them managed their vast enterprises with energy and efficiency. Moreover, when growing infirmity or the accumulation of great wealth blunted their personal aspirations, a surprising number of the early pioneering families were prepared to convert their partnerships into limited companies and, although they retained ultimate control, to transfer the management of their enterprises to a new breed of professionals rather than simply hand the reins to relatively untrained, less highly motivated kinsfolk. Thus it was with the giants of the West of Scotland: Bairds, Merry

& Cunninghame and William Dixon & Company (Corrins, 1974, 292–94; R.D. Corrins, *DSBB*, I, 17–8, 49; Payne, 1979, 74; Payne, 1980, 58; A. Slaven, *DSBB*, I, 34); while in the East, entirely new public companies, such as the Alloa Coal Company, the Fife Coal Company and the Lothian Coal Company appointed trained mining engineers, experienced salesmen and men versed in colliery accounts to manage their concerns from the beginning (M.W. Kirby, M.S. Cotterill and S. Hamilton, *DSBB*, I, 27, 42, 29–30).

Although the number of men employed increased dramatically from about 40,000 in 1866 to 138,000 in 1913, so too did the capital equipment installed to facilitate their labours. Very few innovations in mining practice were ignored, and sound technical reasons can often be adduced to explain cases of slow or partial adoption. On the eve of the First World War, 'in terms of the number of mechanical cutters and conveyors employed at the faces and preparation of output cut by machine, Scotland was far ahead of any other coal-producing district in the UK. Moreover, Scotland was the heaviest user of electricity *below ground*' (Buxton, 1978, 112; Church, 1986, 347). It should be emphasised that this pre-eminence in 1913 was not the result of a sudden, late innovative rush but the consequence of a systematic adoption of new technology since the 1850s (Mitchell, 78; Corrins, 1974, 242, 244–5; M.W. Kirby, *DSBB*, I, 27; Byres, 1967, 254).

Arthur Taylor's belief that 'the predominance of small units [in the coal industry] . . . undoubtedly militated against technical experiment and innovation' (Taylor, 1961, 64), implies that there existed some degree of correlation between the size of the colliery enterprise and technical progressiveness. The scattered data on the Scottish firms tend to lend support to this hypothesis for the estimated share of regional employment of the ten top largest coal producers in eastern Scotland was probably above the national average in 1875 and by 1913 Scotland's coal industry was the most concentrated in Britain (Church, 1986, 400–401). Moreover, many of the largest Scottish firms – the majority of them managerially controlled – did not feel constrained to distribute the bulk of their profits (Church, 1986, 147; Muir, 1952, 1–22; M.W. Kirby, *DSBB*, I, 27).

If it be argued that *selected* cases of technical innovation, profit retention and rapid growth are a misleading guide to regional efficiency (cf. McCloskey, 1971, 290; Buxton, 1978, 112), the evidence of labour productivity is less contentious (Church, 1986, 470–96, and 1989, 15–21). Scotland's performance after 1861 was highly creditable. The labour productivity of the Scottish region was relatively high throughout the fifty years before the First World War, and in its last two decades Scottish mines recorded the highest average output per man-hour (the best measure of productivity) in the United Kingdom (Church, 1986, 472–94), despite the fact that in the west of Scotland output per man was falling rapidly. Here, as Slaven has illustrated, the increasing efficiency of the faceworkers was being more than offset by their need to be supported and sustained by rising numbers of 'oncost' men, thereby reducing the overall output per man employed (Slaven, 1967, 247; Slaven, 1975, 1968).

There was no escaping geology: enhanced costs in Lanarkshire were associated with the exploitation of deeper and thinner seams and lengthening roads to the coal face (Slaven, 1975, 169). By the eve of the First World War, the most modern mines, the largest producing units and the most economic pits were all to be found in eastern Scotland, whose continued development was heavily dependent on the buoyancy of coal sales to northern Europe (Mitchell, 1984, 22). Any objective judgement on the nineteenth century Scottish coal industry must recognise its relative progressiveness. Only with hindsight can ominous signs for the future be perceived: the western district would soon have to contend with a rapid escalation of costs and a collapse of industrial demand, and the prosperity of the eastern areas had become all too vulnerable to the vicissitudes of international trade.

Iron and Steel

The expansion of the Scottish iron industry, inaugurated in the 1830s, continued for four decades. But even before production reached its peak of 1.2 million tons in 1870, the upward momentum was waning. For the next twenty years output fluctuated uncertainly between 0.9 million and 1.1 million tons, fell to approximately 0.6 million in 1894 and, after regaining the 1870 figure in 1902, hovered around 1.35 million tons in the decade before the First World War (Mitchell and Deane, 1962, 131–32). The conjuncture of Neilson's hot blast and the use of blackboard ironstone made possible the production of high quality pig iron at low cost and the Scottish ironmakers came to rely on a modest return on a high turnover, the great bulk of their output being despatched to markets outside Scotland (Birch, 1967, 173). They moved only slowly into the manufacture of wrought or malleable iron (Campbell, 1961–2), apparently convinced that their profits would be maximised by concentrating on smelting.

This opened the way for newcomers to venture into the wrought iron trade. The development of iron shipbuilding provided many opportunities; the requirements of railway construction and the provision of locomotives and rolling stock, while fluctuating wildly, seemed all but inexhaustible (Vamplew, 1969, 72–3); and the needs of engineering concerns in Glasgow and the west of Scotland, busily contracting to build bridges, gasometers and gaswork plant, floating docks and iron piers throughout the world, were of growing importance.

In the 1850s numerous small entrepreneurs promoted a series of malleable ironworks, many of them on or near the banks of the Monkland Canal, close to the source of their raw materials, and their existence encouraged the establishment of works for the manufacture of tubes, tin plate, bolts and rivets (Bremner, 1869, 35–6). For a time there were handsome profits to be made by the puddlers but with the Bessemer process came cheap steel. Bessemer's method of converting pig iron into steel, announced in 1855, excited intense Scottish interest, but the lamentable failure of the initial experiments seemed only to confirm the correctness of the great Scottish iron-makers' concentration on the manufacture of pig iron (Payne, 1979, 19–21; Barraclough, 1990, 40–4). It was left to others to move into steel production.

One firm that did so was the Steel Company of Scotland. Promoted by Sir Charles Tennant, the production of steel at Hallside began in 1873 in a new works equipped with Siemens open-hearth furnaces and rolling mills. Ironically, attempts to utilise 'Blue Billy', a by-product of Tennant's famous chemical works at St Rollox and an important reason for the establishment of the firm, proved abortive and the Steel Company came to rely for its raw materials on external purchases of pig iron and scrap. After a shaky start – the market for steel rails, expected to be its principal product, collapsed in 1874 – the firm quickly diversified its output by going in for ship plates, boiler plates, bars, forgings and steel castings (Payne, 1979, 29–32).

The demand for such products was growing rapidly as the Clyde's ship-builders and engineers became convinced that the greater rigidity, ductility and strength of mild steel made it preferable to wrought iron, and as the price of steel fell, its widespread adoption quickly followed (see below). This was a critical factor in the growth of the Scottish steel industry. Many of the malleable ironmakers, realising that they were faced with a choice between becoming steelmakers or extinction, chose steel. By 1885 over 240,000 tons, or some 40 per cent of the British make of Siemens steel, were being produced by Scottish firms.

However, with the exception of Merry & Cunninghame, who in 1885 put down four basic Bessemer converters at Glengarnock, the old-established Scottish makers of pig-iron once again hesitated. Probably, confronted with growing competition from Cleveland pig iron and the exhaustion of the blackband ores, they decided that their salvation lay not in steel production but in intensifying their activities in coal mining. By the late 1880s the largest Scottish colliery proprietors were all ironmasters (Payne, 1979, 47–54). The result was an almost complete lack of technical integration between the iron- and steel-making sectors of the industry. The thrusting newcomers in steel – the Steel Company of Scotland, David Colville & Sons, malleable iron makers who put down steel furnaces at Dalzell 1880, William Beardmore & Company of Parkhead, and the Lanarkshire Steel Company established in 1889 – did not make iron, and few ironmasters made steel or, if they did, usually conducted the sequential processes in different locations. In addition, a number of other firms in the industry, mainly from a malleable iron-making background, made *neither* pig iron *nor* steel. They simply purchased steel billets and semi-finished steel goods for re-rolling.

This lack of integration, which made the lowest possible costs of production unattainable, was to constitute a serious weakness in the difficult years that followed the First World War. Even more alarming was the industry's increasing dependence on the fluctuating shipbuilding industry. While Scottish steel output doubled between 1885 and 1890, redoubled to almost one million tons by 1900 (representing about 20 per cent of the British total), and rose to nearly 1.5 million tons by 1913, over 70 per cent of its output was destined for the shipbuilding yards of the Clyde, Belfast and the north-east of England (Payne, 1979, 58, 82, 117).

Shipbuilding and Engineering

At the end of the Napoleonic Wars, more than three-quarters of all the wooden sailing vessels built in Scotland came from the east coast yards, principally in Aberdeen and Dundee. The Clyde was unimportant. 'Sixty years later shipbuilding was a complex large-scale heavy engineering industry. Scottish yards built vessels for the world market; ... and the Clyde was already the single most important shipbuilding river in the world' (Slaven, 1981, 353). This transformation rested upon the adaptation of the steam engine for marine propulsion and the replacement of wood by iron in hull construction. These technical changes permitted a vast increase in vessel size and power (Pollard and Robertson, 1979, 9–24) and caused the supersession of small handcraft concerns by firms employing small armies of men, many of whom were dependent for the exercise of their diverse skills upon the use of ingenious power-driven tools and equipment (Hume, 1976, 158–80).

Between 1859 and 1870, Clyde yards launched 70 per cent of all iron tonnage in Britain and two-thirds of all steam tonnage. By 1876, more iron ships were built on the Clyde than in the rest of the world put together (Pollard and Robertson, 1979, 61–2). The tenacious competition of the sailing vessel (Graham, 1956; Harley, 1971) had finally been overcome by the perfection of the compound expansion engine by John Elder and his partner Charles Randolph in 1854 (Moss and Hume, 1977, 37), coupled with the use of improved boilers, the most important of which was James Howden's cylindrical tank, or 'Scotch' boiler, introduced in 1862 (Robb, 1958, 183; Hume, 1954). These developments permitted steamers to capture the majority of the world's long-haul routes in the 1870s (Graham, 1956, 83), when the pace of innovation in shipbuilding and engineering accelerated still further.

'Iron had scarcely established supremacy over timber, when mild steel arrived to replace it' (Cormack, 1929, 150; see also Payne, 1979, 32–6; McCloskey, 1973, 46–54), especially as the price of steel plates fell relative to those of wrought iron (McCloskey, 1973, 50–51). The transition was particularly marked on the Clyde, where between 1879 and 1889 the proportion of steel-built vessels rose from 10.3 per cent to 97.2 per cent, a phenomenal development unequalled by any other shipbuilding region of Britain (Cormack, 1929, 150).

Meanwhile, striking engineering advances continued to be made. Steel water-tube boilers permitted higher pressures and resulted in greater thermal efficiency. Higher pressures, in turn, made possible the triple expansion engine, designed by Alexander Kirk, then of John Elder & Company and first fitted in the ship *Propontis* in 1874. The ultimate step in the search for power and economy in the reciprocating steam engine was taken in 1885, when Walter Brock of Dennys devised quadruple expansion utilising Scotch boilers working at about 220lb per square inch, or twenty times the working pressures common only forty years earlier (Robb, 1958, 182–4; Guthrie, 1971, 116–33).

Yet this apparently most successful of industries possessed characteristics dangerous for the wellbeing of the Scottish economy and had itself developed disquieting weaknesses (Campbell, 1980, 60–68). Shipbuilding was dependent upon a highly volatile demand, which was transmitted to the iron and steel industry and thence to many other sectors of the Scottish economy (Pollock, 1905, 172), producing fluctuations with a greater amplitude than those affecting other regions of Great Britain. They had a major influence on the structure of the industry and the choice of production techniques employed by its constituent firms.

Despite the growing complexity and rapidly rising value of the final product, the small-scale, independent family firm retained its importance, perhaps because its capital needs were relatively modest. The volatility of demand for ships acted as a disincentive to fixed investment and confirmed the rationality of labour-intensive production techniques. These enabled the shipbuilders to minimise overhead costs and to transfer many of the financial burdens associated with downswings in the cycle to the skilled labour force, which could readily be laid off (Pollard and Robertson, 1979, 28–9; Reid, 1980, 29, 43). The combined effect of these influences and strategies was that most shipbuilding firms remained relatively small and independent. The level of concentration was low and even the large yards were unable to achieve significant economies of scale (Lorenz and Wilkinson, 1986, 110–11).

Although individual shipbuilders could do little to stabilise demand, they could try to ensure good order books in an increasingly competitive market by taking shares in, forming alliances with, or even promoting shipping lines (Moss and Hume, 1977, 88–9). But once 'into shipping' several of the great Clyde builders, such as the Dennys and Lithgows, discovered that more money could be made by operating ships than by building them (Slaven, *DSBB*, 1986, 229; Robertson, 1974, 36–47; Laird, 1961). Where these connections resulted in specialisation and a heavy dependence upon a small group of customers, they carried with them their own dangers. A special case of this dependence occurred when a number of builders, such as John Browns of Clydebank and the Fairfield Shipbuilding and Engineering Company (successors to Randolph & Elder), became deeply involved in fulfilling the demands of the Admiralty, thereby making their own continued prosperity partially a function of public policy which proved to be even more erratic than the customary vicissitudes of shipbuilding (Campbell, 1980, 61; Peebles, 1987, 30–87).

The increasingly precarious prosperity of shipbuilding on the Clyde is most apparent in the profit records of many yards. Many vessels went down the slipways bringing nothing but substantial losses to their builders (Peebles, 1990, 42–3). To some extent this was inevitable, given the lengthy gestation period between ordering and launching and the differing variability of cycles in freight rates and the costs of the shipbuilders' major inputs, labour and materials (Pollard and Robertson, 1979, 27–8). More significant than the simple existence of periods of 'profitless prosperity' is the fact that the percentage of contracts that resulted in losses seems steadily to have increased over time. By the eve of the First World War, shipbuilding on the Clyde 'was not conspicuously profitable even in its most active days' (Campbell, 1980, 65), a state of affairs partially to be explained by intense competition from the north-east of England, a region which since the 1880s had launched even more ships than the Clyde (Pollard and Robertson, 1979, 62–4, 252–3).

Thus beneath much of the prosperity of the Scottish heavy industries at the beginning of the twentieth century were symptoms of industrial malaise. The future might not have been so bleak had there developed a more diversified and less export-dependent range of metal-using industries. There were some notable successes – as in the manufacture of sugar machinery, structural engineering and, most notably, in locomotive engineering (Moss and Hume, 1977, 27–36, 42–62) – but too many of these activities were dependent for their long-term prosperity on shipbuilding or on railway construction overseas. Even those engineering shops that had rushed to meet the growing demands of essential components of bridges, railways and rolling stock, had lost much of their dynamism by the 1880s. Much of Scottish industry had probably come to rely upon collusion in place of competition. For example, no sooner had the Anderston Foundry established some new product – steel sleepers in the 1880s, tunnel segments in the 1890s, or tramway fittings in the 1900s – than trade associations developed to regulate the market (Hargrave, 1991).

Collusion appears to have been endemic in the iron industry (Campbell, 1961, 312–6). Everywhere manufacturers sought to manage markets in their own interests, allotting fixed quotas to members, penalising those who overproduced to compensate those who underproduced. Small firms were thereby able to survive, but the attainment of economies of scale, the recruitment of better educated, more technically proficient and adventurous management, and the development of modern management practices were inhibited. Effective diversification was discouraged and economic growth retarded. Many firms established in mid-century had by its close come to be 'more interested in dividing the cake than in baking a new, larger, one' (Hargrave, 1991, 175).

Even where the attempt *was* made – in motor cars – it ended in dismisal failure, written off as 'hopeless' as early as 1921 (Campbell, 1980, 166). By the eve of the First World War, of the fifty or so companies established to make cars in Scotland since 1896 (MacDonald and Browning, 1961), the most promising, Argyll, had almost withered away (S.C. Orr, *DSBB*, I, 259–60; Bloomfield, 1981, 134–38; Lewchuck, 1987, 118; Adeney, 1980, 59–60) and Albion had abandoned motor cars in favour of commercial vehicles (McKinstry, 1991). Only Arrol Johnston seemed to be secure. But this too was a mirage, for a controlling interest in Arrol Johnston had been acquired by William Beardmore in 1902 and, following the war, William Beardmore & Company, grotesquely distorted by its efforts to expand armament manufacture, was to collapse, bringing down the entire group of companies with which Sir William was associated (Hume and Moss, 1979, 51, 160–61, 224).

There is no easy explanation for this failure in motor cars. Arguments that rest upon the inhospitable business and technical atmosphere of Scotland for car manufacture lack conviction. Although the Scottish economy did not generate the range of suppliers of component parts and finishings that were to make the English midlands so attractive a location (Checkland, *DSBB*, I, 251–52), the great majority of the early Scottish car firms apparently disappeared because of poor management: costing systems were primitive, capital investment was either recklessly profligate or inadequate, after sales service was ignored, and no thought appears to have been given to the provision of spare parts. But perhaps the greatest mistake was to assume that only the wealthy were likely to want, or to be able to purchase cars. Only Alexander Govan of Argyll had a vision of a potential mass market and he died prematurely. Few shared his insight, even in England, and it is significant that of the 400 or so *British* car makers that entered the industry before 1914, relatively few survived (Saul, 1962, 23), and that of the indigenous concerns only Austin and Morris grew large enough to exploit the economies of scale before the early 1930s (Church and Miller, 1977). The size of the British market provided room for but one or two mass producers. The fact that before 1930 there was no Scottish firms among them may be ascribed to luck rather than to any particularly antagonistic features of Scottish culture or to any technical inability among Scottish engineers. Nevertheless, having failed to get into the mass production of cars in the early days of the industry, it became progressively more difficult to enter the industry. After 1930 any newcomer was faced by barriers that were all but unscalable.

II

The First World War and Its Aftermath
1914–1939

Coal

Most authorities are emphatic that the impact of the First World War on the Scottish coal industry was unfavourable, and that the industry emerged from the war 'gravely impaired' (Buxton, 1978, 159; Scott and Cunnison, 1924, 48), most obviously in the 'almost complete collapse' of exports. These fell from 10.4 million tons – representing about one-quarter of total output (42.5 million tons) – in 1913 to 2.4 million tons in 1918 and to a pitiful 1.3 million tons in 1920. But were not the problems of a purely temporary nature, destined with the return of peace quickly to be solved by market forces and hence to constitute a mere blip in the inexorable upward climb experienced in the pre-war era? At first, it was possible to think in such terms (Campbell, 1980, 154), but optimism proved to be misplaced. Scotland was unable to benefit in the post-war boom largely because continuing state control of the coal industry maintained a price structure which discriminated against the countries that Scotland had traditionally supplied (Supple, 1987, 120; Buxton, 1978, 161–2). Even more important, from the mid-1920s, aggregate demand for coal ceased to grow, held in check by many economies in its use, especially by iron and steel producers. Moreover, the market for coal was seriously affected by the growing substitution of gas, electricity and oil in the home and in industry (Slaven, 1975, 196).

There had been downswings in coal sales before and there was little about the sharp fall of 1925 to distinguish it from its predecessors. It was believed therefore that its malign effects could be ameliorated and its direction reversed by the traditional method of reducing costs, the single most important element in which was wages. But as a minimum level of wages seemed to have been guaranteed by the complex settlement which had ended the bitter strike of 1921 and had been reaffirmed by a further agreement in 1924, industrial conflict was inevitable. When the mine owners insisted on cutting wages and increasing the length of the working day, the miners, initially supported by the General Strike called by the TUC, struck and stayed out for a period of seven months. The struggle left a legacy of embittered industrial relations. What was particularly tragic was that the reduction of wages failed to solve the industry's problems. The remorseless downward pressure on prices made coalmining essentially a profitless activity from 1927 to the mid-1930s (Slaven, 1975, 197; Buxton, 1979, 66).

If wages could be squeezed no further, the more progressive owners sought to reduce total costs by continuing to install more mechanical equipment. 'During the 1920s, Scotland established a real lead in every branch of the new technology of the industry with a percentage of output mechanically cut and conveyed that was never less than *twice* as high as that in Britain as a whole', and 'throughout the inter-war years the productivity of labour in Scotland remained, . . . higher than in any other district with the one exception of Yorkshire', a district which enjoyed much more favourable geological and underground conditions than Scotland (Buxton, 1970, 480, 482–85). An important contributory factor to the relatively high and sustained labour productivity was the high level of concentration in Scotland. In 1930 three-quarters of the total output of the district [31.7 million tons] came from a mere 20 colliery companies (Buxton, 1970, 488), and even these were linked by interlocking directorates (Scott and Hughes, 1980, 85–6). This unification of ownership and control facilitated the implementation of a policy of constant modernisation (Supple, 1987, 311n, 368) and in developing the new colliery at Comrie, Charles Reid of the Fife Coal Company set new standards of coal production both underground and on the surface (W. Reid, *DSBB*, I, 61). Nor were marketing arrangements neglected by some of the leading figures in the industry. In 1934 Sir Andrew Nimmo successfully inaugurated 'a scheme for the central regulation of sales in order to overcome the problem of mounting competition in the home market between inland and exporting districts' (M.W. Kirby and S. Hamilton, *DSBB*, I, 58), and in the same year James Hood of the Lothian Coal Company and R.T. Moore of Edinburgh Collieries attempted to rationalise coal marketing among a group of collieries in the east by establishing the Associated Lothian Coal Owners Ltd. (M.S. Cotterill, *DSBB*, I, 45).

If Scottish colliery companies in the inter-war periods were so progressive, why were profits so elusive until the late 1930s? The answer lies in the demand for their product. As Buxton has explained, 'the price of coal per ton raised in [Scotland] remained well below that of the other [major] regions [except Northumberland]. By the early 1930s the average price per ton of Scottish coal amounted to only 80 per cent of that in Great Britain as a whole and to a mere 52 per cent of the top selling price available for anthracite . . . in South Wales' (Buxton, 1979, 68–9). These lower selling prices for the major grades of Scottish coal were 'more than sufficient to destroy any relative advantage to be gained from greater efficiency . . . The prosperity of the Scottish coal industry ultimately depended upon forces well beyond the individual's ability to control' (Buxton, 1970, 487).

Faced with such intractable difficulties, it is all the more remarkable that between the wars Scotland retained an almost constant share of about 13.5 per cent of Britain's annual coal production. Yet there was a fall in both the output of coal and the numbers employed. The highest output was 38.5 million tons in 1923, less than in any of the pre-war years since 1905, and even a recovery of output in the 1930s attained a peak of only 32.3 million tons in 1937. Employment fell even more dramatically, from 155,000 in 1920, to 81,600 in 1933. In 1937, the best year of the 1930s, only 90,600 were employed. 'Whatever the achievements of the industry, it was in decline' (Campbell, 1980, 116).

Iron and Steel

Despite a sixfold increase in the output of steel since 1885, there were disquieting structural and locational weaknesses present in the Scottish iron and steel industry in 1914. They were exacerbated by policies adopted to meet the demands of the war and the post-war boom. The immediate effect of the war was to increase Scottish steel-making capacity and to concentrate control of the industry. David Colville & Sons acceded to the appeals by the Ministry of Munitions to increase the output of steel by taking over the Clydebridge Steel Company and the Glengarnock Iron and Steel Company and by putting down new plant. Outside Colvilles the most important increase in melting capacity was the extension of Beardmore's Mossend plant, specifically to make shell bars and ship plates. Such was the overwhelming importance of Clyde shipbuilding that the extensions planned and executed for Scotland were, in the national context, disproportionately large (Burn, 1940, 358–62; Hatch, 1919, 41). It is noteworthy too that due to the exigencies of war the *nature* of the steel made in Scotland changed. The shipbuilders' insistence that only acid open hearth steel would meet their requirements gave way to a reluctant acceptance of basic steel. From less than 20 per cent of Scottish total steel output in 1913, the share of basic steel rose to about 60 per cent in the late 1920s and to 75 per cent by 1937/38 (Buxton, 1976, 108–9; Payne, 1979, 179, 129). Yet this increase in the production of basic steel was not matched by a corresponding growth in the output of basic iron, and Buxton has argued that 'it was the inability of producers to maintain supplies of basic pig . . . that constituted the *principal weakness* of the iron and steel industry in Scotland . . . the ratio of basic pig to basic steel output fell from 37 per cent in 1913 to only 8 per cent in 1920/1 and to 7 per cent by 1937/8' (Buxton, 1976, 108–9, emphasis supplied).

It was not the task of the Iron and Steel Department of the Ministry of Munitions to rectify imbalances in productive capacities that had grown up before hostilities began, nor had it any duty to ease the eventual transition to peacetime conditions. Hence, while Scottish steel-making capacity was substantially enlarged, not a single new blast furnace was built in Scotland. In the light of its rapidly declining resource base (Slaven, 1975, 169–70), this neglect of smelting was understandable, but it meant that Scotland emerged from the war with the imbalance in its iron and steel industry exacerbated and the lack of integration between iron and steel reinforced (Gibson, 1958, 38; Campbell, 1980, 118–19).

The other major change that stemmed directly from the war concerned the ownership of the Scottish steel industry. It was believed that the end of hostilities would be followed by a massive shipbuilding programme as owners tried to make good the heavy wartime losses in order to exploit the expected renewal of international trade. Confident of full order books and conscious of the many competing demands for steel, the shipbuilders were anxious to safeguard their supplies of ship and boiler plates and heavy forgings. The consequence was a scramble by the shipbuilders to acquire control of the Scottish steel makers. Within two years, with the exception of the Clydeside Works of Stewart & Lloyds at Mossend, the entire steel-making capacity of Scotland was in the hands of the shipbuilders (Payne, 1977, 162, 166).

The sudden collapse of the post-war boom meant that both the ship-builders and their steel interests were plunged into depression. No matter who *owned* the Scottish steel works, most of their products were destined for the shipyards: the health of the Scottish steel industry was determined by fluctuations in ship construction (Payne, 1979, 147–50). This linkage explains the relatively poor performance of the industry during the inter-war years. From the trough of 1921, the revival of Scottish steel output was sluggish; production throughout the 1920s remained well below the record level achieved at the beginning of the decade. Even in the relatively good years of the latter half of the 1930s output remained on average about half a million tons below that of 1920.

To the extent that the Scottish steel industry was dependent upon ship-building for its market, its relative stagnation during the inter-war period was beyond its control. It is also clear that the decline of smelting acted as a positive incubus on the steel-making and iron-founding trades and, indirectly, on all the metal-using industries of the Glasgow conurbation (Gibson, 1958, 38). The ironmasters might have imported the necessary grades of iron ore to offset the progressive exhaustion of native reserves but for the anachronistic location of the industry and the obsolescence of its plant. The costs incurred in the assembly of raw materials at inland sites were relatively high, and their conversion into pig iron was carried out in hand-charged, lilliputian blast furnaces barely one-third of the optimum size recommended in the late 1920s (Scott and Cunnison, 1924, 45). Nothing less than the creation of modern blast furnace capacity, preferably on a tidewater site, was required and in the depressed conditions of the inter-war period this was not feasible.

The steelmakers had to look elsewhere for their raw materials. They found supplies of basic pig iron in England, the Continent and India, but above all they replaced it altogether by using increasing quantities of cheap scrap, until by the 1930s the ratio of scrap to pig iron in the burden of the average Scottish open hearth furnace was 2:1, a far higher proportion than was the practice elsewhere in the UK (Buxton, 1976, 110–12). The consequence was the virtual, if temporary, extinction of the Scottish iron industry. Only six of a total of 83 furnaces were in blast by the end of 1930, and in the latter half of the following year, only Carron Company was making pig iron.

If the steelmakers could not look to the smelters for salvation, they themselves might have taken appropriate remedial action by merger, followed by the concentration of output in the most modern plant, supplemented by re-equipment. Of all the recent studies of the industry, that by Tolliday provides the most comprehensive and convincing explanation of why this did not take place. He emphasises the multi-layered ownership of the steel industry. Crudely put, the steel companies were owned by the shipbuilders, who themselves were heavily indebted to the banks (including the Bank of England) and, because of loans through the Trade Facilities Act, to the Treasury. In seeking to protect their own interests, these creditors pursued policies which rarely, if ever, were congruent with vigorous restructuring, a situation exacerbated by profound conflicts of interest between creditors, shareholders, family groups and customers *within* the individual firms. The result was almost total paralysis (Tolliday, 1985, 92–109).

The only scheme to emerge in the 1920s that addressed the fundamental issue of the future productive capacity of the Scottish steel industry largely foundered on the rock of these competing sectional interests (Payne, 1979, 170–80). In December 1928 Lord Weir (C.W. Munn, *DSBB*, I, 197–8) convinced the leading figures in the industry that they should consider 'the possibilities of a single unit for the production of Iron and Steel in Scotland'. It was agreed that H.A. Brassert & Company, an internationally-known firm of consulting engineers, should make a full investigation and submit recommendations. Brasserts found that the old splint coal blast furnaces operated by Bairds at Gartsherrie, Dunlops at Clyde Iron and Colvilles at Glengarnock, should be scrapped and that *only* a fully integrated iron- and steel-making plant on the Clyde equipped with the most modern dock facilities would permit the rehabilitation of Scotland's iron and steel industry.

After a careful examination, the Brassert scheme was rejected. However convincing its technical excellence, it was calculated that it would produce annual net savings of only £160,000. The force of the Brassert proposals was seriously weakened by the offer by the Tata Iron and Steel Company of Calcutta to deliver pig iron to Colvilles for the foreseeable future at a price even less than the cost of production envisaged for the new tidewater plant (Payne, 1979, 181). Furthermore, such were the market conditions during the following two to three years that the necessary investment might have brought them all to their knees. For all that, a most favourable opportunity to restructure the Scottish steel industry had been lost (Warren, 1965, 36; ·Tolliday, 1987, 108–109).

There was no alternative but to push ahead with less ambitious schemes. It was believed that some economies and greater efficiency might result from a simple merger of the Scottish steel makers. Even the pursuit of this lesser objective revived all the fears and suspicions that had inhibited action throughout the previous decade, but eventually a new company, Colvilles Ltd., came into being in 1931 to acquire the Dalzell, Clydebridge and Glengarnock Works from David Colville & Sons and the Clyde Iron Works and the Calderbank Steel Works from James Dunlop & Company, together with their associated collieries. At last, a beginning had been made, and although 'it did little to advance the technical reorganisation of the Scottish industry that Brassert had deemed essential . . . it brought together the financial power of the Lithgow group [which owned Dunlop & Co.] with the productive strength of Colvilles' (Tolliday, 1987, 108). By 1936, this combination had taken over Stewart & Lloyds' plate business in Scottish and in world export markets, purchased the Mossend Works of William Beardmore & Company, bought the Steel Company of Scotland and absorbed the Lanarkshire Steel Company (Payne, 1979, 180–217). With these acquisitions, Colvilles controlled over 80 per cent of Scottish steel production.

Unity of ownership was one thing; the reorganisation of productive facilities to attain the maximum economies of scale was another. Such was the severity of the depression that it was unrealistic to expect the resuscitation of the Brassert proposals. Instead, under the supervision of Andrew McCance (P.L. Payne, *DSBB*, I, 116–18) a programme of relatively inexpensive improvements and patching operations was carried out at all the works, culminating in the modernisation of the Clyde iron-works and linking them by means of a bridge across the Clyde with the Clydebridge steelworks. The results were lowered conversion costs and impressive gains in productivity as McCance's brilliant improvisations enhanced the beneficial effects of a fuller use of available capacity as demand at last improved after 1936.

By the eve of the Second World War, the relative inefficiency of the Scottish iron and steel industry had been reduced. And yet, as Kenneth Warren has repeatedly argued, was not this a case of where 'the better was the enemy of the best? . . . By the end of the 1930s Scottish steelworks were still more completely dependent on scrap than those of any other district except Sheffield. Only Clydebridge used hot metal, and the bulk of steel capacity, some distance away from modern blast furnaces in mid-Lanark-shire, was still confined to cold practice. Colvilles remained large importers of pig iron, and Scotland had become more dependent on imported ores than the other seven iron-making districts [of Great Britain] . . . There had been considerable progress in the 1930s in modernising the Scottish steel industry, but there still seemed to be a place for a tidewater works at a new deep-water location' (Warren, 1965, 87–8; Warren, 1969; Warren, 1979, 121–22).

Shipbuilding

The fundamental problem confronting the shipbuilding industry between the wars was *chronic* overcapacity in relation to potential demand. This produced difficulties of such magnitude that to maintain that the industry should have reformed itself during the inter-war years is unrealistic (cf. Barnett, 1986, 110–14). The experiences of 1920–38 ossified the practices and shaped the attitudes that contributed to the virtual demise of Scottish shipbuilding after the Second World War (Pagnamenta and Overy, 1984, 124–36).

The rapid reduction of this industry, *apparently* so prosperous in 1913, to despair and long-term decline can be explained to some extent by the malign impact of the war itself. During the conflict the equivalent of some 30 per cent of the world's pre-war merchant fleet was lost, and it was the expectation of a replacement boom that produced the frenzied expansion of capacity in the immediate post-war years. By 1920 the number of berths in British yards exceeded the 1914 figure by nearly 40 per cent (Slaven, 1981, 125, 140). Not only British shipbuilding capacity was enlarged, so too was that of the United States, Japan, Holland and the Scandinavian countries. By 1920 the world's total shipbuilding capacity – about five million gross tons in 1913 – had been doubled. The immediate consequence was a rapid increase in world mercantile tonnage from 49.1 million tons in 1914 to 65.2 million tons in 1923 (Balfour Committee, IV, 1928, 376–77, 398, 405).

In marked contrast to this expansion of carrying capacity, world trade barely grew, and a collapse of freight rates ensued. The consequence was a diminution in the output of the industry from its world peak of 6 million tons in 1920 to an average of barely two million tons between 1924 and 1938. Since the shipyards of the United Kingdom *alone* had an annual capacity of well over three million gross tons, British yards could have produced the whole of the new tonnage launched in the world in every year between the wars and still have had capacity to spare (Slaven, 1981, 126; Balfour Committee, IV, 1928, 383–85; Parkinson, 1979, 79–80).

But, of course, not all of the new orders came to Britain. Whereas tonnage constructed for non-British owners averaged about 20 per cent of output in the quinquennium before the war, it fell substantially short of that level for the latter halves of both the 1920s and 1930s, and British shipbuilders became increasingly dependent on a depressed home market. Moreover, naval orders, which between 1899 and 1913 had constituted the equivalent of some 15 per cent of all tonnage launched in Britain, fell rapidly after the Armistice in 1918 and ceased entirely with the signing of the Washington Treaty for the Limitation of Naval Armaments in 1921. Not until the very eve of the Second World War did naval tonnage approach its pre-1913 significance (Slaven, 1982, 41–2; Peebles, 1987, 139, 165–66).

In such an environment there were more shipyards than would be needed in the foreseeable future. Yet although the yards were idle, only a handful went bankrupt and were eliminated by market forces. This tenaciousness was rooted in individualism and family pride, sustained by reserves accumulated in better times, and made easier to bear by relatively modest and heavily depreciated capital stocks. But even the most individualistic of the shipbuilders recognised that the survival of the industry demanded a degree of co-operation and the elimination of some part of its surplus capacity. It was the warship builders – who had received virtually no orders since 1921 – who 'first ran for cover', to use Slaven's phrase. Early in January 1925 they devised a rota system to share out work. Three years later the merchant and warship builders inaugurated the 'Shipbuilders Conference', which quickly evolved the principles under which redundant berths could be eliminated. With the support of the Bank of England, National Shipbuilders Security Ltd. was created in 1930 to purchase and close down shipyards that were redundant or obsolete. Within three years 35 per cent of Scotland's total tonnage capacity – about half a million tons – had been 'sterilised'.

But although the scheme *reduced* 'the potential for reckless price cutting by too many order-hungry yards', it did little to rationalise the industry. No series of mergers or further concentration followed, and the Second World War put an end to proposals stemming from the Shipbuilders Conference that might have led to an extension of the activities of NSS and the implementation of more far-reaching plans. (The foregoing discussion draws heavily on Slaven, 1981a; see also Hume and Moss, 1979, 214–18). It is surprising that in a period during which weak demand stimulated the search for cost savings, and appallingly heavy unemployment and unsuccessful strikes weakened the resistance of skilled workers, the shipbuilding employers did not redesign the productive process and 'deskill' the work force. This question has been directly addressed by McKinlay who explains that market constraints – the irregular composition and volatile nature of the demand for ships – acted as a disincentive to capital investment and mechanization, deterred product standardisation and encouraged the maintenance of organisational flexibility through the continued use of skilled labour (McKinlay, 1986, 220).

So it was that the terrible events of the inter-war period did little to alter either the fragmented industrial structure or the working customs and practices that shipbuilding had inherited from the nineteenth century. As Parkinson observed, 'the industry failed, perhaps only partly through its own fault, to lay the foundations of a change from being builders of fine ships to being managers of fine shipyards' (Parkinson, 1979, 98). It was to prove a fatal legacy.

Textiles

While Scotland's heavy industries were grappling with problems of unprecedented severity, the various branches of the textile trades experienced mixed fortunes. Cotton continued its irreversible decline. Both the Clyde Spinning Company and the Glasgow Cotton Spinning Company were liquidated by disappointed English speculators who had taken them over in the post-war boom. By 1937 there were only four or five spinners left, though J. & P. Coats soldiered on.

With over 12,000 workers in 1930, Coats was the largest employer in Scotland, concentrating on the manufacture of domestic and industrial thread at their Ferguslie mills and mercerised embroidery and specialised handicraft threads at the Anchor Mills. When it became apparent that costs of production at the 'Home mills' were relatively high compared with other mills in Europe, Coats recast their managerial structure, moving away from the highly centralised system of functional control developed under Philippi (who died in 1917) towards one of geographical divisions, each of which was encouraged to devolve more power to the group's subsidiary companies. Coats also introduced new managerial techniques first adopted in their American mills. Although these methods raised productivity, they confirmed that costs at Paisley were relatively high. Nevertheless, Coats' directors, conscious of heavy unemployment in Clydeside, maintained a higher level of production in Scotland than was justified on cost grounds. By 1938 the Home mills, still employing over 10,000 millworkers, were generating about one-third of the group's total sales, of which no less than 80 per cent was exported. Profits and dividends may have fallen during the 1930s, but this was no mean record (J.B.K. Hunter, personal communication; J.B.K. Hunter, *DSBB*, I, 364–66).

Although cotton spinning had largely disappeared by the eve of the Second World War, there were still numerous weavers, many of them specialising on fine muslins, overwhelmingly for export. The largest of these, D. & J. Anderson, revealed an acute sensitivity to market conditions and a willingness to innovate, but they brought their family firm little reward. Andersons survived until 1959, but it was a profitless survival (A.J. Robertson, *DSBB*, I, 305–7; Oakley, 1937, 230–31). Others – such as David Lean & Sons and Walter Henderson Ltd. – were more financially successful, but they lasted no longer. Nor did the United Turkey Red Company. Despite extensive re-equipment and diversification, and the application of its methods of dyeing to wool, silk and man-made fibres, the company – which in its heyday had employed over 5,000 workers in the Vale of Leven – never recovered from the major slump of the early 1920s, the retirement of John Christie, and the widespread use by its competitors of a new dye, Napthol Red. In 1960 the company's assets were purchased by the Calico Printers' Association, and the Alexandria Works were closed (N.J. Morgan, *DSBB*, I, 322–3; Tarrant, 1987, 47).

Things were little better in Dundee. Hostilities once again stimulated the jute industry, called upon to produce sand bags by the million, but in the long-term this reversal of the pre-war trend towards finer goods was highly detrimental for it involved an element of technical retrogression. Coupled with a temporary inability to supply foreign markets, it encouraged the establishment of local industries and resulted in a permanent loss of trade.

After the short-lived post-war boom, the industry was characterised by 'tumbling prices and a declining demand', with unemployment in the early 1930s exceeding 50 per cent of the work force. The industry's response was amalgamation and rationalisation. In October 1920 a number of firms – including Cox Brothers – came together to form Jute Industries Ltd., and four years later another grouping resulted in the establishment of Low & Bonar. But this increase in concentration – so often seen as *the* solution to British industry's predicament – failed to generate recovery. Both employment and Dundee's international competitiveness continued to decline (Howe, 1982, 12–3).

Had it not been for the relative prosperity of linoleum and carpets, the manufacture of which required jute backing, Dundee might have experienced even greater suffering. Nairns of Kirkcaldy did particularly well. An increase in its capital to well over £2m permitted an expansion in both its range of products and its worldwide production, sales and distributive network by means of a series of mergers and trading agreements, and the firms's dividends averaged well over 12 per cent throughout the inter-war period (N.J. Morgan, *DSBB*, I, 377–79; Muir, 1956, 109–29). Some part of this prosperity was due to the universal use of linoleum, the housing boom of the 1930s and the rising standard of living available to those in employment, but it is evident that these favourable circumstances were skilfully exploited by Sir Michael Nairn, the third generation of the family to run the business. It is possible too that the domination of the industry by a mere handful of firms – of which Nairn's Kirkcaldy neighbour, Barry, Ostlere & Shepherd was one – permitted the implementation of informal price codes and common trade practices among the members of the British Federation of Linoleum Manufacturers and, after 1934, the Linoleum Manufacturers' Association (Evely and Little, 1960, 278–0).

The manufacturers of carpets too benefited from membership of trade associations, and Stoddards strengthened their position by merger, absorbing Ronald Jack & Co. of Paisley and the Caledonian Carpet Company of Stirling in 1918 (Stoddard, 1962, 9). Like the manufacturers of linoleum, the carpet makers were able to take advantage of buoyant home demand for their products, especially in the 1930s when the house building boom offset declining international competitiveness (Bartlett, 1978, 190–1). But the principal Scottish firms did more than simply react to favourable market trends. Templetons were responsible for product and technical innovations, being first in the field with a full range of seamless Spool Axminsters in 1925, introducing Gripper Axminster in 1929, and developing the Hook Wilton loom in the 1930s (Cunnison and Gilfillan, 1958, 249–50; Young, 1944, 61–4), while Blackwood Morton & Sons installed the most modern looms from America and Germany in entirely new premises in Kilmarnock (J. Mair, *DSBB*, I, 372).

While the carpet industry was steadily expanding, the manufacture of woollen fabrics ceased to grow. Only those firms, such as Patons of Alloa and Fleming, Reids, who had already moved into the production of worsted yarns, appear to have prospered during the inter-war period. Many firms were wound up and those that survived did so largely because they no longer made any allowance for the depreciation of their antiquated machinery or because, at last, they were forced to strengthen themselves by grouping together, sometimes with English firms (Gulvin, 1973, 189). Indeed, Patons themselves merged with J. & J. Baldwins of Halifax to form the largest woollen-yarn spinning company in Great Britain, Paton & Baldwins Ltd., in 1920 (N.J. Morgan, *DSBB*, I, 389); and William Hollins of Nottingham, the makers of Viyella yarns and fabrics, continued to do much of their weaving in Glasgow, having taken over two Glasgow mills at the turn of the century (Oakley, 1937, 231; Wells, 1968, 104).

The most successful textiles sector was hosiery and knitwear which, by constant adaptation to the vagaries of the market and remarkable feats of diversification, enjoyed some measure of growth throughout the inter-war period. None of the firms was very large, measured by paid-up capital, but this branch of textiles remained one in which relatively small-scale operation was economically viable, even essential. 'The high-class Hawick trade demanded personal attention and flexible market response' (Gulvin, 1984, 95) to accommodate to the rapidly changing dictates of fashion. There was a constant need to maintain a balance between the production of underwear and outerwear, and success demanded endless permutations in designing, styling and the use of colour. The pricing of the product involved the exercise of careful judgement in order to exploit different market conditions at home and overseas; and the creation and maintenance of brand names called for imaginative advertising and marketing techniques. Not surprisingly, some errors were made, particularly in timing the introduction of new product lines, and there was some evidence of over-capacity, but several firms, such as Lyle & Scott and Robert Pringle, made modest profits and by the end of the period they or their products had become household names (Gulvin, 1984, 87–119).

So it was that textiles continued to play a substantial role in the Scottish economy.

Collapse and Revival under New Management
1939–1990

Coal

On the eve of the Second World War, the Scottish coal industry was in a precarious condition, its continued existence dependent upon indigenous geological resources that were fast running out or becoming increasingly costly to exploit. Ominously, output per man in Scotland, for decades higher than the figures for England and Wales, fell below the latter for the first time during the quinquennium ending 1950. At the same time the cost of coal-getting in Scotland came to exceed the average cost in England and Wales by an increasing margin. Part of the explanation for this relative loss of ground lay in the fact that between 1935 and 1951 other colliery districts had caught up and surpassed Scotland's pre-war superiority in mechanisation, but another factor was the relatively small size of the Scottish collieries, the average annual output from which had by 1951 become the lowest for any colliery district in Britain (Leser, 1954, 115–7).

Thus in 1947 when the mines were nationalised and subjected to detailed examination, it was decided to phase out more than half of those in Scotland. To compensate for the consequent annual loss of output, estimated at some 7 million tons, and to raise Scotland's annual coal production to the 30 million tons that forward projections indicated would be required to meet domestic and export demand, the National Coal Board proposed to embark on an ambitious programme of new sinkings, to develop new surface drift mines and to reconstruct and modernise nearly 40 pits, mainly in the eastern coalfield.

The hopes underlying the *Plan for Coal* were to be cruelly shattered; the assumptions built into the *Plan* were exposed as utterly mistaken. When, after a decade of rising demand, the market for coal collapsed in the late 1950s, the prop supporting the NCB's £200m investment programme for Scottish coal suddenly gave way. The shift towards the use of oil, gas and electricity between 1955–66 resulted in the consumption of coal in Scotland falling by over 25 per cent to 16 million tons, only half that anticipated. As oil almost doubled its share of primary fuel consumption between 1963 and 1970 and the use of natural gas and nuclear power rose, the NCB accelerated the closure of uneconomic pits, reduced open-cast mining and ran down the labour force. But labour productivity remained substantially below the national average, despite a massive investment in coal-cutting machinery and power-loading equipment.

This low productivity contributed to the higher production costs in Scottish pits, and to help the Scottish Division reduce its deficit on sales the NCB instituted a special regional surcharge on Scottish coal. The imposition of higher coal prices merely accelerated the substitution of alternative fuels by both domestic and industrial consumers. Had the state-owned electricity industry not been prevailed upon to consume large and increasing amounts of coal, the Scottish coal industry might have succumbed two decades ago. In 1955 power stations in Scotland consumed 3.15 million tons of coal, or nearly 15 per cent of the coal raised, by 1961 the proportion so used was nearly 20 per cent, a figure that had more than doubled by 1970 and more than tripled by 1975 (67.2 per cent).

Despite continued rationalisation, a favourable pricing policy, and special arrangements guaranteeing massive purchases of coal by Scottish power stations from 1977 (Johnston *et al.*, 1971, 110–111; Ashworth, 1986, 381–82), the Scottish coal industry was incapable of making a profit. During the 1960s Scotland was responsible for almost half the total deficiencies recorded by the operating divisions of the NCB, and although Scotland's share of the deficits did fall, the losses per ton of saleable coal during the late 1970s and early 1980s remained more than double the national average. The area losses could not be ascribed to the operation of a few very uneconomic pits: *all* Scotland's collieries were uneconomic in the period 1976/1977 – 1980/1981 (Payne, 1985, 90–91).

Although Kerevan and Saville (1985) have criticised the NCB's accounts and have argued that they give a misleading picture of the operating costs of individual pits, the annual deficits made by the Scottish collieries bring into question the future of the coal industry in Scotland. In the past decade, the number of active pits has fallen from 15 to one and the labour force from nearly 20,000 to less than 2,000. Two faces at the Longannet complex in Fife are producing coal for firing Scottish Power's neighbouring thermal generating station. But when existing politically-motivated contracts with the newly privatised electricity company expire, it seems doubtful whether Scottish Power will continue to purchase Longannet's deep-mined coal at prices substantially higher than those on world markets, especially when the Scottish Office is insisting that the electricity company spend nearly £400m on equipping its power stations with flue gas de-sulphurisation equipment (*Times*, 10 May 1991). And if Longannet goes, there will be nothing left of an industry which only forty years ago produced 23 million tons of coal, employed 83,000 men and contributed one eighth of Britain's coal output.

Iron and Steel

In the past three decades, detailed comparative studies have shown that the long-term success or even the survival of a nation's steel industry depends upon fully integrated works on tidewater sites and, at the risk of

37

over simplification, it could be argued that the extinction of the Scottish steel industry was inevitable after the rejection of the Brassert scheme in 1929 and the refusal of Colvilles Ltd. to countenance its rehabilitation in 1944–47. There were very good reasons for Colvilles' post-war decision (Payne, 1979, 284–305). Their careful estimates of future demand, the current availability of coking coal, pig iron and scrap, and the firm's sense of social responsibility towards those whose livelihoods depended on existing works, convinced Colvilles that they should persevere with a more 'practical' programme of modernisation, the centrepiece of which was the creation of the Ravenscraig complex in the late 1950s. But the disastrous long-term consequences of this fatal decision were exacerbated by the government's insistence that Colvilles erect a strip mill at Ravenscraig while simultaneously 'awarding' another strip mill to Llanwern in South Wales.

As Sir Andrew McCance had predicted, there was insufficient demand for the high-quality light strip and sheet steel produced by the mill, the capital cost of which, combined with severe undercapacity working meant that when Colvilles was nationalised (for the second time) in 1967, the group was technically bankrupt. Were disaggregated figures available, they would probably reveal that the Scottish iron and steel industry has worked at a loss ever since. Certainly, the rare glimpses of comparative costs afforded by the accounts of the British Steel Corporation indicate that the losses per ton of finished steel production in Scotland were far higher than those of any other steel-making area in Great Britain, reflecting the relatively smaller scale, the lower proportion of capacity utilisation and the higher cost of fuel in Scotland. When heavy freight charges per unit of finished output are added to these losses, the pressures upon the BSC to close down what was left of Colvilles' heritage are understandable. Only the political power of the Scottish lobby prevented Sir Ian MacGregor from doing so in the early 1980s.

Although the fortunes of the BSC were to be transformed by ruthless economies, its Scottish component, despite an increase in productivity and efficiency, continued to be regarded as the Corporation's weakest geographical division, and its strip mill as 'the most likely casualty' in the event of further rationalisation, repeatedly reprieved only by intense political pressure. When the privatisation of steel took place in December 1988, the Scottish steel industry was doomed. The power and influence of the Scottish lobby was irrevocably weakened. If Ravenscraig could be run only at a loss, it should be closed. And this, of course, is what happened. In April 1991, the hot strip mill ceased production. Only some facilities for steelmaking and continuous slab casting remain, and recent reports indicate the meagre prospects for their commercial future. In 1977 more than 13,000 men had been employed in steel-making in Lanarkshire; in July 1991 there were only 1,200. If not yet extinct, the Scottish iron and steel industry is in a terminal condition, weakened by the exhaustion of indigenous raw materials, emasculated by the collapse of shipbuilding and condemned to a lingering death by what can now be seen as past errors of judgement (Payne, 1979; Payne, 1985, 93–101; Warren, 1969).

Shipbuilding

Of the 49 companies building ships in Scotland in 1938, 39 had been in continuous existence throughout the inter-war period. Of these companies the great majority were owned and controlled by a dominant family (Slaven, 1980). The virtual disappearance of the shipbuilding industry may be a direct consequence of this structure (Payne, 1985, 101). In the third quarter of the twentieth century, a period during which world launchings of merchant tonnage increased ten-fold, the output of Scottish yards remained well below the figures attained even during the 1920s. In absolute terms, British tonnage – of which Scottish yards consistently contributed between a quarter and a third – did not so much decline as fail to rise. Thus the 1.3 million tons of shipping launched from British yards in both 1950 and 1975 represented 38 per cent of world launchings at the earlier date but less than 4 per cent 25 years later. Faced with uniquely favourable demand conditions, British and Scottish output remained stagnant, seemingly tethered to a little over one million tons.

If demand was so buoyant, the constraints on output must have been rooted in supply factors. Initially, the shipbuilders could argue that they received inadequate allocations of steel, but there was also an exasperating shortage of skilled labour, particularly of experienced welders, and this in turn inhibited the expansion of pre-fabrication. But pre-fabrication techniques involved heavy capital expenditure and more systematic use of plant than was usual on the Clyde (Cairncross, 1958, 239). This was the essence of the long-term problem. The majority of the fiercely competitive Clyde yards hesitated to raise the capital required for fundamental changes in the methods of construction or to recruit specialists to senior positions since both courses of action would have eroded familial control and disrupted customary working practices. If the employers had been reluctant to impose a new discipline on their employees in the inter-war period, when the men's power was negligible, they were even more reluctant to do so in the post-war years when the bargaining power of the work force had been greatly strengthened.

The need for radical change grew even more imperative with the rise of the tanker. Tankers are simpler vessels than the Clyde's traditional output, and their construction offered fewer opportunities for the exercise of the craft skills of the work-force. A major competitive advantage enjoyed by the Scottish shipbuilders was thereby significantly reduced. Their comparative position deteriorated still further with the evolution of *giant* tankers and bulk carriers for the building and launching of which their crowded riverside locations were totally unsuitable. Change was inhibited even by the sheer scale of the post-war boom. Anything which might disrupt maximum immediate production – which the creation of better yard layouts and the introduction of flow-line methods and new managerial techniques threatened to do – was to be avoided.

The result was the petrification of Scottish shipbuilding at a level of development increasingly inappropriate for the rapidly changing conditions of the post-war era. And so, when the market lost its buoyancy in the late 1950s, the Clyde was ill-equipped to grapple with the severity of inter-national competition. For a time, the builders were sustained by the loyalty of British shipowners, but when the lower quotations and shorter and more reliable delivery times of Continental and Japanese builders undermined that loyalty, their last support crumbled. Thenceforth, British shipbuilding survived only with the assistance of the state.

By the mid 1960s many of the famous Clyde builders had gone and the Geddes Committee, appointed to examine the industry, predicted that the rest would shortly follow unless its detailed recommendations were rigorously implemented. (For the Geddes Committee, see Slaven, 1980). It was too late. Despite the grouping of yards, the creation of the Shipbuilding Industry Board and the award of massive grants and loans, the industry stumbled from crisis to crisis, and the proportion of the world's shipbuilding launched from British yards declined to reach a figure (c.3.8 per cent) in the mid-1970s, less than half that of the Geddes Committee's most pessimistic estimates.

The nationalisation of the industry in 1977 – just two years after the collapse of the post-war boom in shipbuilding – confirmed the inability of British yards to survive without continuous injections of public funds. The last of the Scottish heavy industries had passed into the hands of the state, but even this failed to preserve it. In 1979–80 about half of the £110 million losses incurred by British Shipbuilders was attributed to Scottish yards. There was no alternative but to run down the labour force – many of whom willingly co-operated by making 'a massive rush for redundancy' – and abandon the yards. One by one they closed. Now only a handful remain, kept alive by subsidies, Admiralty contracts, and the government's assumption of their debts and losses. On the Clyde, only Yarrows (now owned by General Electric Co.), who specialise in warships, and Kvaerner Govan (acquired from British Shipbuilders by the Norwegian company in August 1988) maintain a precarious existence.

Textiles

The post-war history of the textile industry has also been one of relative decline. In the process the leading firms have huddled together in defensive mergers and are now merely components of huge multinational groupings. Although many of the famous names have been retained, the firms them-selves have lost their independence, ultimate ownership and control often residing in the hands of institutional investors domiciled outside Scotland. Only the most optimistic would regard the transformation as being beneficial to the long-term survival of this sector of Scottish industry.

Let us look briefly at J. & P. Coats, for so long the sole surviving reminder of a glorious past. By the end of the 1950s the thread market was stagnating, the firm's profits were declining rapidly and, if growth was to be maintained, diversification was believed to be essential. Coats chose to go into wool. They already had a 25 per cent interest in Fleming, Reid & Company, whose retail chain had expanded to 300 'Scotch Wool Shops'. The other 75 per cent of Fleming, Reids was owned by Paton & Baldwins, whose products had for some time been distributed through Coats' Central Agency. A union of the two firms promised to bring advantages to both of them. Furthermore, by being taken over by Coats, Paton & Baldwins would be less vulnerable to absorption by Courtaulds, who were rapidly acquiring over a third of Lancashire's spinning capacity and a host of textile, hosiery and garment manufacturers (Singleton, 1991, 220–28).

Coats Paton came into existence in 1960. After an hiatus of five years, spent grappling with problems of assimilation, the new firm began to strengthen its position in the woollen industry and to move closer to the consumer. In 1965, it took a controlling interest in Pasolds; in 1966, it bought the Bellman chain of wool and clothing shops, intending to use Bellman's management to pull round the Scotch Wool Shops, whose sales had been seriously affected by the onward march of Marks & Spencers; and in 1967 it acquired Jaeger, whose retail outlets were principally supplied by the group's own factories (Turner, 1969, 413).

These acquisitions were intended to protect Coats Paton's position in the market from Courtaulds. There were others in the field, similarly motivated. One such was ICI. Anxious to ensure a market for its synthetic fibres, ICI fostered the growth of a number of textile firms, two of which, Viyella International and Carrington & Dewhurst, merged to form Carrington Viyella, in which ICI held a 35 per cent share. Subsequently, Carrington Viyella merged with Vantona and in 1986, in an agreed bid which valued Coats Paton at £734 million, Vantona Viyella took over Coats Paton. With this merger the control of much of Scotland's textile industry passed into the hands of Coats Viyella.

This sequence of events is important because of its possible consequences. The rationalisation of the textile industry by Courtaulds, Coats Viyella, Tootals and the Dawson group (see below) over the past three decades has not halted the decline of British textiles. Indeed, several firms are becoming increasingly reliant on what they euphemistically call their 'marketing and sourcing strengths'. In other words, they are abandoning production and assuming the role of merchants, buying or having fabrics and garments made to their own specification in India, Malaysia, Hong Kong and Singapore (Chapman, 1991, 185). The implications for Scottish textiles are extremely worrying. Coats Viyella – whose principal subsidiaries include

J. & P. Coats, Paton & Baldwins, Jaeger Holdings and William Hollins, each of which, in turn, controls numerous Scottish firms – is attempting 'to minimise the adverse effects of changes in economic conditions by relocating manufacturing capacity' to low-cost countries or 'by sourcing from them' (Sir David Alliance, quoted by Chapman, 1991, 186).

The other major components of the textile industry – jute, linoleum, carpets, hosiery and knitwear – hold little more promise than cotton, thread and wool. During the Second World War, as in the First, the jute industry experienced a period of exceptional demand. As early as 1945, however, its prospects were recognised as being gloomy, but no one could have predicted the severity of the subsequent contraction. Due to the continuation of import regulations instituted during the war to protect Dundee producers from Indian competition and the industry's own trade pricing agreements, at first all went well. There was, furthermore, an unexpected boost to the demand for jute by the advent of tufted carpets, the makers of which originally used jute as a backing material. But it proved to be a false dawn. Activity in jute peaked in the mid-1950s when 39 firms were in the trade and 19,000 were employed. Since then the industry has experienced unremitting decline, suffering from the substitution of multiwall paper bags for jute sacks; the development of bulk-handling methods for grain and other products and the introduction of bulk containerisation; the collapse of the linoleum market and, worst of all, the arrival and rapid adoption of a synthetic fibre, polypropylene, as a jute substitute.

Howe's study (Howe, 1982) of the industry's reaction to this succession of blows: rationalisation by means of mergers and acquisitions, the development of vertical integration, and wide-ranging diversification, is highly illuminating, but even Howe was unable to forsee that in the following decade the jute industry would almost disappear. In 1988 only twelve firms were left and even these had survived only by moving into industrial and engineering textiles based on polypropylene fabrics. Within ten years the jute industry had become 'virtually unrecognisable', its labour force reduced to less than one thousand workers (*Industrial Growth Scotland*, 2nd edition, 1989, 426).

Not the least of the woes afflicting jute was the sudden disintegration of the linoleum industry. For ten years after the war, output of linoleum rose to an annual peak of 51.6 million square metres in 1955. This level of production was sustained until the end of the decade. Demand then fell off rapidly to less than 10 million sq. metres in 1969 and to a seventh of this figure (1.4 million sq. metres) in 1980, after which production was too low even to record in the *Annual Abstract of Statistics*. Nairns of Kirkcaldy, who once dominated the industry has meanwhile been taken over by the Swiss multinational Fabro AG.

In contrast, the carpet industry experienced boom conditions after the war, the growth in demand being attributable to a low level of unemployment, rising real incomes and substantial residential building. Yet, as the industry's historian has said, 'a considerable part of the increase in the consumption of carpets in the United Kingdom must be attributed to major technical changes in the industry itself. The most striking change was the introduction of tufted carpets, . . . manufactured by a process quite different from the traditional Brussels, Wilton, Tapestry, Chenille and Axminster carpets' (Bartlett, 1978, 191). The tufting process originated in America and was introduced into the UK in 1952. Production on a significant scale began a few years later when five carpet makers, including Templetons, formed a consortium to produce tufted carpets under the brand name of 'Kosset'.

Thereafter, progress was rapid. Sales were encouraged by low prices made possible by the simplicity and speed of the tufting process and the use of man-made fibres substantially cheaper than wool. By 1970 production of tufted carpeting exceeded that of the traditional types of carpets whether woven with wool or man-made fibres. Scottish firms had been in the vanguard of this development. Templetons were soon joined by Stoddards and Blackwood Morton & Sons, who had established new plants in 1961 (Hart *et al.*, 1973, 41). By the late 1960s the industry was suffering from excess capacity. The response was a round of mergers accelerated by Viyella's purchase of the facilities created by the innovative Cyril Lord who, in establishing a unique distribution system of direct selling, over-reached himself and crashed in 1968 (Rhys David, *DBB*, III, 854; Hart *et al.*, 1973, 42).

Rising sales of relatively inexpensive tufted carpets halted and reversed the post-war upward trend in sales of traditional carpets, and several of those makers who still retained a heavy commitment to Brussels, Wilton, Axminster and Chenille carpets also sought refuge from intense competition in merger. In 1968 Templetons merged with Gray's Carpets and in the following year the combine was taken over by the multinational Guthrie Corporation, anxious to reduce its dependency on overseas rubber, tea and palm oil plantations. By 1970 the Guthrie group, A.F. Stoddard (then part of Stoddard Holdings) and Blackwood Morton were among the eleven firms responsible for over 75 per cent of woven carpet production. The process of rationalisation and growing concentration continued as tufted carpeting captured an increasing share of the floor-covering market. Blackwood Morton, having established Thistletex Carpets Ltd. in 1967, plunged into the ancilliary processes of spinning and dyeing, and expanded its felt-making plant in Kilmarnock, but went into receivership in 1981 (J. Mair, *DSBB*, I, 373). By the end of the 1980s, the Guthrie Corporation had become a subsidiary of the British Belting and Asbestos Group, and the ownership of Templetons had passed into the hands of Stoddard Sekers International, a holding company which had gained control of the majority of Scotland's remaining carpet manufacturers. At the end of the decade Stoddard Sekers, whose subsidiaries included Lyle Carpets Ltd. and Henry Widnell & Stewart, had a market value of £22m and was regarded as being simply 'a small carpet maker' (*Investors Chronicle*, 7 December 1990, 58).

Although some part of the recent history of knitwear has already been alluded to, the sequence of events in this branch of Scottish textiles deserves some elaboration. (The subsequent paragraphs draw heavily on Gulvin, 1984, 120–38.) During the war much of the capacity of the hosiery and knitwear industry was closed down and a large proportion of the labour force either mobilised or redeployed. Post-war recovery was rapid, but growth was not sustained: a peak in 1956 was followed by a decade of stagnation and, after 1971, steep decline. By 1979 real gross output was barely one third of the level of 1965 and the workforce had fallen from 20.4 thousand to 14.7 thousand.

During this period the tendency for woollen underwear to be supplanted by fancy woollen outerwear continued and hosiery almost ceased to be produced. In the Borders, activity came to be dominated by a few large concerns of which in the early 1960s the most important was Pringle of Scotland (as Robert Pringle & Sons had become in 1959) and Lyle & Scott. Pringle's growth had largely been based on its sales of light cashmere cardigans and jerseys and its expansion into men's fashion wear, and Lyle & Scott's on its highly successful Y-front underwear. By contrast, Braemar Knitwear Ltd. had grown by merger with Ballantyne Bros. of Peebles and Turner, Rutherford & Co. after the three firms had been taken over in 1961 by Hugh Fraser's Scottish & Universal Investments Ltd. with the object of promoting their branded goods by the House of Fraser (Moss and Turton, 1989, 199). But the continued success of all the firms came increasingly to depend upon the use of expensive, high speed, semi-automatic machinery. To purchase this required tapping new sources of capital and usually necessitated the conversion of many of the private concerns into public limited companies. This made them vulnerable to takeover and loss of autonomy and the traditional pattern of family control and restricted shareholdings rapidly gave way to large groupings and institutional investment (Gulvin, 1984, 133).

In the middle 1960s the Baird group took control of Braemar and Ballantynes, formerly owned by Hugh Fraser, and created Scottish Border Cashmere; Wolsley purchased Lyle & Scott and were themselves acquired by Courtaulds; and Jaeger took over James Renwick of Hawick, only a year before being purchased by Coats Paton. Meanwhile, Alan Smith, of the Kinross firm of yarn spinners, Todd & Duncan, had gained control of the cashmere processors, Joseph Dawson & Co. of Bradford, and purchased both Laidlaw & Fairgrieve of Galashiels and Pringle of Scotland, the largest and most prestigious of the fashioned knitwear manufacturers. By the end of the decade the Dawson group controlled a large proportion of the Border knitwear industry (including Scottish Border Cashmere), but by wildly diversifying into merchant banking and leisure investments had over extended itself. During the sharp economic recession of the 1970s, Dawsons was forced to re-structure and to close many of its plants. The Ballantyne Spinning Company (part of Scottish Border Cashmere) was shut down and much of Pringle's capacity was reduced (Gulvin, 1984, 134–37).

That this unhappy outcome was not simply a consequence of ownership by the over-stretched Dawson group is, however, apparent from the similar trading experience of the largest surviving independent firm, Peter Scott. It was only the smallest firms – with modest capitals – that came through the sharp recession of the 1970s comparatively unscathed, and even they have suffered greatly over the last decade, during which many firms have closed and hundreds of jobs have been lost. Only Pringle of Scotland is doing well, having updated its product range and enjoyed great success with its extensive collection of golf clothing. To try to ensure the industry's continued survival nine of the remaining Borders producers are currently drawing up a strategic plan which focuses on marketing, investment and training initiatives. It is believed that the greatest threat in the future will come from Taiwan, Korea and China, and that the Italians, with greater government support than the Borders, have already overtaken Scotland in innovative design (*Sunday Times* (Scotland), 28 July 1991; *Daily Telegraph*, 19 August 1991).

'Dramatic Gestures' and Recent Developments

As the staple industries continued their decline, 'dramatic gestures' – Nicholas Morgan's phrase (Morgan, 1988, 1352) – were made to stay the consequential reduction in employment. All too often they ended in recrimination and bitter disappointment. The strip mill at Ravenscraig was intended to attract new firms to Scotland and to permit the more rapid expansion of those existing concerns that used high quality light steel strip: 'firms making refrigerators, stoves, clocks, vacuum cleaners and other household electrical equipment, a large range of typewriter, cash register, and accounting machines . . . , electronic devices, electrical switchgear, possibly railway carriages and so on' (Sir Robert MacLean, quoted Payne, 1979, 374). But, above all, it was hoped that the local availability of sheet steel would bring about the re-birth of motor manufacture. And so it did, but it was not a spontaneous birth. By a mixture of financial inducements, government pressures and the refusal of Industrial Development Certificates for expansion in more favoured locations, the British Motor Corporation was persuaded to transfer the production of heavy goods vehicle from Birmingham to Bathgate and, even more significant, the Rootes group agreed to gamble over £20 million in building a factory to produce the Hillman Imp at Linwood.

Both ventures – conducted throughout their brief lives in a blaze of publicity – were to end in tragedy: transplanted organs rejected, despite repeated surgery, by the economic body. Plagued by industrial disputes, vitiated by the inexperience of the management and the labour force, and burdened by fundamental design faults in its products, Linwood helped to bring the Rootes group to its knees, was used as a bargaining counter by the American Chrysler Corporation (who gained control of Rootes in 1967), and finally closed in 1981 by the French giant Peugeot Citroën, its final owners, whose motive for acquiring the plant was seen by many as being to gain access to the British dealer network (for the complex story see Hood and Young, 1982, 61–80). Two years later, less dramatically but just as finally, Bathgate closed, a victim of world-wide depression in the commercial vehicle market.

Other major government-inspired initiatives were no more successful. The British Aluminium Company's smelter at Invergordon – regarded as a growth node which would breed new enterprises – came to grief in 1981, victim of high fuel costs and a collapse in the world price of the metal (Morgan, 1988, 1355; Payne, 1988, 252–53). In the same year, Wiggins Teape's pulp mill at Corpach, Fort William, closed down after fifteen years of operation made profitless by technological problems, market difficulties and unexpectedly high raw material costs. Even some of the huge American multinational companies were 'in retreat' from Scotland in the late 1970s. Goodyear's tyre plant at Drumchapel, praised by the President of the company in 1957 as the best factory of its kind in the world, was 'rated at the bottom of the totem pole in just about every respect' when it was shut down in 1979. Monsanto closed its nylon plants at Dundonald and Cumnock in Ayrshire in the same year, and Singers their great factory at Clydebank in June 1980. Other multinationals, such as Hoover, Timex, Massey-Ferguson and SKF, shed tens of thousands of jobs between 1976 and 1988 (Hood and Young, 1982, 29–30, 42–60, 141–45; McDermott, 1988, 151–66; Industry Department for Scotland, November, 1988, 7–8).

But this emphasis on failure and retreat – a peculiarly British phenomenon more highly developed in Scotland than in any other region of the United Kingdom – is misleading. Alongside the much publicized failures, there have been notable successes. In the last three decades Scottish manufacturing has become much more diversified; its industrial structure now closely resembles that of Great Britain as a whole (Buxton, 1985, 47; Randall, 1985, 254; Meredith, 1990, 69). The fact that the creation of new jobs has been on a scale insufficient to maintain past levels of employment in manufacturing is a reflection of the greater capital intensity of the new activities and the slow growth of the British economy as a whole.

To a considerable extent this more balanced economy has been dependent upon foreign capital and enterprise (Industry Department of Scotland, November, 1988). This has brought its own problems. As Buxton succinctly observed: 'Foreign investment is notoriously fickle, particularly where it assumes the form of branch-factory creation with headquarters remaining firmly in the country of origin. Moreover, it is essentially footloose and can be quickly withdrawn when economic conditions are unpropitious or because of factors quite unrelated to the actual performance of the branch firm [as in the Caterpillar company's withdrawal from Uddingston in 1987 (Haworth, 1987, 67)]. Frequently, too, closures, are effected with little regard for the region which originally welcomes such incoming capital with inducements and concessions' (Buxton, 1985, 47–8).

These very real dangers should occasion no surprise. The Toothill Report warned against them thirty years ago. What was needed, Toothill argued, was large-scale and integrated industrial complexes, generating substantial internal economies, and firmly embedded in Scottish soil (Sims and Wood, 1984, v). For all the undoubted recent success of Scottish industry, this has not happened or, if it has, it has occurred only to a limited extent. The hopes of the Scottish Development Agency and its predecessors that as companies settled in Scotland, indigenous supply companies would sprout up around them and, having become well established, would provide research and develop new products, is as yet unfulfilled (Randall, 1985, 255–56).

Let us glance at two recent developments. Electronics has been one of Scotland's success stories currently employing over 46,000 people in over 400 companies (Industry Department for Scotland, February, 1988; Meredith, 1990, 74). The sector embraces microchips, personal computers, defence electronics, and some of the fastest growing specialities in tele-communications. Firms concerned in this development are Motorola and Digital of the United States, National Semiconductor and NEC of Japan, and GPT, a company combining GEC and Plessey. So far the manufacturing operations of these giant multinational companies have eschewed local design and product development – a thriving indigenous electronics industry remains a dream. (For more evidence of this, see Gallagher and Miller, 1991, 46, 49).

What then of North Sea Oil? This is not the place to analyse the impact of North Sea Oil on the Scottish economy, far less to disaggregate its impact on Scotland's industrial sector. Suffice it to say that the construction, equipping and installation of offshore petroleum structures represents the largest capital expenditure by private enterprise in British (and certainly Scottish) history, generating orders totalling nearly £14,000 million between 1972 and 1989 (Pike, 1990, 2). Huge construction yards sprang up, seemingly overnight, in Scotland. Yards at Ardersier and Nigg Bay, in the Inverness area, and at Methil, on the Firth of Forth, built steel platforms, as did lesser yards at Stornoway and Dundee. Yards for the construction of concrete platforms were built at Loch Kishorn and Ardyne Point. The activity was frantic; the expenditure enormous. But the contribution to the manufacturing sector of the Scottish economy has been disappointing. The reasons for this are highly complex, but among them may be mentioned the established contractual patterns within the international petroleum industry; and prolonged inability of many British firms to meet the specifications demanded by the industry; and, in the crucially important early years, a general apprehension among Scottish industrialists and their financial backers that North Sea oil was a mere 'flash in the pan' and the massive capital expenditure necessary to exploit the bonanza far too risky to contemplate (Pike, 1990).

This is not to deny the profound impact that North Sea oil has had on the labour market, particularly in the Grampian Region, nor to diminish the overall economic importance of North Sea oil. It is simply to emphasise the relatively minor influence that the exploitation of the oil of the United Kingdom continental shelf has had on Scotland's – and indeed Britain's *manufacturing* sector. (For the position in 1980, see McDowall, 1985, 306.) There has been an influx of American-owned concerns (e.g. Brown & Root, Baker Oil Tools and McDermotts) and their arrival has greatly boosted the share of Scottish industry controlled from the United States – of all the regions in Britain, Scotland has by far the largest proportion of US-owned subsidiary companies – but the oil industry has not yet put down real roots in the Scottish economy to create significant and permanent backward linkages. And if it has not done so by 1990, it seems improbable that it will ever do so.

Is it possible to draw any conclusions from this brief and selective survey of Scottish industry? What emerges most clearly is the growing rapidity of change. The great staples that dominated the Scottish economy for over a century are gone, although the speed of their departure was slowed by collusive agreements and the actions of the state in providing protection, massive injections of capital, and the life support system of nationalisation. Meanwhile, many branches of textiles and engineering have survived and have been supplemented by the growth of electrical and electronic engineering, the manufacture of office machinery and data processing equipment, and an expansion of chemicals and man-made fibres. The evolution of this more balanced *structure* has been wholly beneficial. Indeed, the hopes of those who proclaimed the need for just such a transformation would seem to have been fulfilled in the past two or three decades. But the individual units that together make up this re-invigorated manufacturing sector seem more fragile, more transient, than what has gone before. This is why the imminent closure of Ravenscraig, for example, has produced such a furore, for underlying the demands that Scotland retains its steel industry is an implicit belief that once established, a specific location has an inalienable right to continue to do what to many it seems always to have done. In an international economy characterised by accelerating change, such rights no longer exist. They are being swept away by the pace of technical change, the growing economies of scale, and the changing locus of ownership and control.

Industry in Scotland *is* more healthy that it has been for generations but it is no longer *Scottish* industry. In 1913 Scotland could be said to possess a distinctive semi-autonomous economy. During the course of the twentieth century, this became assimilated into first the British economy and then the international economy, and one corollary of this evolution has been that a great number of Scottish firms have either lost their independence or, in the case of branch plants, have never possessed any. The majority of the larger enterprises are now units of national or international groupings, controlled not from Glasgow, Motherwell and Hawick, but from London, Houston and Tokyo, and dependent for their survival not on their own productivity or even profitability but on the value of their contribution to the global strategy of vast multinational companies. This is the reality which no amount of nationalist fervour or nostalgic sentiment can reverse.

SELECT BIBLIOGRAPHY

In preparing this study, the sector essays and the individual biographies that make up the *Dictionary of Scottish Business Biography*, edited by A. Slaven and S. Checkland (Aberdeen: Vol. 1, *The Staple Industries*, 1986; Vol. 2, *Processing, Distribution, Services*, 1990), have been so valuable that references to this source, which is cited *DSBB* followed by the number of the volume, are preceded by the names of the authors. *DBB* refers to the *Dictionary of Business Biography*, edited by D.J. Jeremy, 5 vols. (London, 1984–6).

M. Adeney, *The Motor Makers* (London, 1988).

W. Ashworth, *The History of the British Coal Industry*. Vol. 5: *1946–1982. The Nationalized Industry* (Oxford, 1986).

[Balfour] Committee on Industry and Trade, *Survey of Metal Industries* (London, 1928).

C. Barnett, *The Audit of War* (London, 1986).

K. Barraclough, *Steelmaking: 1850–1900* (London, 1990).

J.N. Bartlett, *Carpeting the millions: the growth of Britain's carpet industry* (Edinburgh, 1978).

A. Birch, *The Economic History of the British Iron & Steel Industry* (London, 1967).

G.T. Bloomfield, 'New integrated motor works in Scotland 1899–1914', *Industrial Archaeology Review*, V, 1981.

D. Bremner, *The Industries of Scotland* (Edinburgh, 1869). Reprinted 1969.

A.J. Youngson Brown, 'The Scottish Coal Industry, 1854–1886'. Unpublished D.Litt. thesis, Aberdeen, 1953.

D. Burn, *The Economic History of Steelmaking, 1867–1939* (Cambridge, 1940).

J. Butt and K. Ponting, eds., *Scottish Textile History* (Aberdeen, 1987).

J. Butt and J.T. Ward, eds., *Scottish Themes* (Edinburgh, 1976).

N.K. Buxton, 'Entrepreneurial Efficiency in the British Coal Industry between the Wars', *Economic History Review*, Second Series, XXIII, 1970.

N.K. Buxton, 'Efficiency and organization in Scotland's Iron and Steel Industry during the Interwar Period', *Economic History Review*, Second Series, XXIX, 1976.

N.K. Buxton, *The Economic Development of the British Coal Industry* (London, 1978).

N.K. Buxton, 'Coalmining', in Buxton and Aldcroft, eds., *British Industry*, 1979.

N.K. Buxton, 'The Scottish Economy, 1945–79: Performance, Structure and Problems', in Saville, ed., *Economic Development of Modern Scotland* (1985).

N.K. Buxton and D.H. Aldcroft, eds., *British Industry between the Wars* (London, 1979).

T.J. Byers, 'Entrepreneurship in the Scottish Heavy Industries, 1870–1900', in Payne, ed., *Studies in Scottish Business History*, 1967.

A.K. Cairncross, ed., *The Scottish Economy* (Cambridge, 1954).

A.K. Cairncross, 'The Economy of Glasgow', in Miller and Tivy, eds., *The Glasgow Region*, 1958.

A.K. Cairncross and J.B.K. Hunter, 'The early growth of Messrs J. & P. Coats, 1830–83', *Business History*, XXIX, 1987.

R.H. Campbell, 'Statistics of the Scottish Pig Iron Trade, 1830 to 1865'. *Proceedings of the West of Scotland Iron and Steel Institute*, LXIV, 1956–7.

R.H. Campbell, *Carron Company* (Edinburgh, 1961).

R.H. Campbell, 'Early malleable iron production in Scotland', *Business History*, IV, 1961–2.

R.H. Campbell, *Scotland since 1707: the rise of an industrial society* (Oxford, 1965).

R.H. Campbell, *The Rise and Fall of Scottish Industry, 1707–1939* (Edinburgh, 1980).

R.H. Campbell, A.A.M. Duncan and D. Dunnett, eds., *The Story of Scotland* (Glasgow, 1987–1988).

S. Chapman, 'Mergers and takeovers in the postwar textile industry: the experience of hosiery and knitwear', *Business History*, 30, 1988.

S. Chapman, 'The decline and rise of textile merchanting, 1880–1990', in M.B. Rose, ed., *International Competition and Strategic Response* (London, 1991).

R. Church and M. Miller, 'The Big Three: Competition, Management and Marketing in the British Motor Industry, 1922–1939', in B. Supple, ed., *Essays in British Business History*, 1977.

R. Church, *The History of the British Coal Industry. Vol. 3: 1830–1913. Victorian pre-eminence* (Oxford, 1986).

R. Church, 'Production, employment and labour productivity in the British coalfields, 1830–1913: some reinterpretations', *Business History*, XXXI, 1989.

P.L. Cook, 'The Calico Printing Industry', in P.L. Cook and R. Cohen, *Effects of Mergers* (London, 1958).

D.S. Cormack, 'An Economic History of Shipbuilding and Marine Engineering (with special reference to the West of Scotland)'. Unpublished Ph.D. thesis, University of Glasgow, 1929.

R.D. Corrins, 'William Baird & Company, Coal and Iron Masters, 1830–1914'. Unpublished Ph.D. thesis, University of Strathclyde, 1974.

J. Cunnison and J.B.S. Gilfillan, eds., *The Third Statistical Account of Scotland: Glasgow* (Glasgow, 1958).

D. Daiches, ed., *A Companion to Scottish Culture* (London, 1981).

Departmental Committee on Shipping and Shipbuilding, *Shipping and Shipbuilding Industries after the War* (London, 1918 [Cd.9092]).

B. Elbaum and W. Lazonick, eds., *The Decline of the British Economy* (Oxford, 1986).

R. Evely and I.M.D. Little, *Concentration in British Industry* (Cambridge, 1960).

C. Gallagher and P. Miller, 'The Performance of new firms in Scotland and the South East, 1980–87', *The Royal Bank of Scotland Review*, No. 170, June 1991.

E. Gauldie, *The Dundee Textile Industry 1790–1885* (Edinburgh, 1969).

I.F. Gibson, The establishment of the Scottish steel industry', *Scottish Journal of Political Economy*, V, 1958.

G.S. Graham, 'The ascendancy of the sailing ship 1855–1885', *Economic History Review*, Second Series, IX, 1956.

C. Gulvin, *The Tweedmakers: A History of the Scottish fancy woollen industry 1600–1914* (Newton Abbot, 1973).

C. Gulvin, *The Scottish Hosiery and Knitwear Industry* (Edinburgh, 1984).

J. Guthrie, *A History of Marine Engineering* (London, 1971).

J.F. Hargrave, 'Competition and collusion in the British railway track fittings industry: the case of the Anderston Foundry, 1800–1960'. Unpublished Ph.D. thesis, University of Durham, 1991.

C.K. Harley, 'The shift from sailing ships to steamships, 1850–1890 . . . ', in McCloskey, ed., *Mature Economy*, 1971.

P.E. Hart, M.A. Utton and G. Walshe, *Mergers and concentration in British industry* (Cambridge, 1973).

F.H. Hatch, *The Iron and Steel Industry of the United Kingdom under War Conditions* (London, 1919).

N. Haworth, 'Making Tracks: Caterpillar's crawl from Scotland', *Quarterly Economic Commentary of the Fraser of Allander Institute*, XII (1987).

John Hood, compiler, *The History of Clydebank* (Carnforth, Lancs., 1988).

N. Hood and S. Young, *Multinationals in Retreat. The Scottish Experience* (Edinburgh, 1982).

W.S. Howe, *The Dundee Textiles Industry 1960–1977. Decline and Diversification* (Aberdeen, 1982).

C.W. Hume, *A Hundred Years of Howden Engineering* (Glasgow, 1954).

J.R. Hume, 'Shipbuilding Machine Tools', in Butt and Ward, eds., *Scottish Themes*, 1976.

J.R. Hume and Michael S. Moss, *Beardmore. The History of a Scottish Historical Giant* (London, 1979).

Industry Department for Scotland, *Statistical Bulletin* No. C1.2, 'The Electronics Industry in Scotland' (February 1988).

Industry Department for Scotland, *Statistical Bulletin* No. A3.2, 'Overseas Ownership in Scottish Manufacturing Industry' (November 1988).

T.L. Johnston, N.K. Buxton and D. Mair, *Structure and Growth of the Scottish Economy* (London, 1971).

G. Kerevan and R. Saville, *The economic case for deep-mined coal in Scotland* (Mimeo, 1985).

J. Kuuse and A. Slaven, eds., *Scottish and Scandinavian Shipbuilding Seminar: Development Problems in Historical Perspective* (Glasgow, 1980).

D. Laird, *Paddy Henderson. A History of the Scottish Shipping Firm P. Henderson & Co., 1834–1961* (Glasgow, 1961).

B. Lenman, C. Lythe and E. Gauldie, *Dundee and its Textile Industry* (Dundee, 1969).

C.E.V. Leser, 'Coal-mining', in A.K. Cairncross, ed., *The Scottish Economy* (1954).

W. Lewchuk, *American technology and the British vehicle industry* (Cambridge, 1987).

E. Lorenz and F. Wilkinson, 'The shipbuilding industry, 1880–1965', in Elbaum and Lazonick, eds., *Decline*, 1986.

D.N. McCloskey, 'International differences in productivity? Coal and Steel in America and Britain before World War I', in McCloskey, ed., *Mature Economy*, 1971.

D.N. McCloskey, ed., *Essays on a Mature Economy: Britain after 1840* (London, 1971).

D.N. McCloskey, *Economic Maturity and Entrepreneurial Decline: British Iron and Steel, 1870–1913* (Cambridge, Mass., 1973).

H.W. Macrosty, *The Trust Movement in British Industry* (London, 1907).

M. McDermott, 'Singer: Competition and Closure', in Hood, comp., *History of Clydebank*, 1988.

A. McKinlay, 'Employers and skilled workers in the inter-war depression: engineering and shipbuilding on Clydeside 1919–1939'. Unpublished D.Phil. thesis, University of Oxford, 1986.

A. McKinlay, 'The Inter-War Depression and the Effort Bargain: Shipyard riveters and the "Workman's Foreman", 1919–1939', *Scottish Economic and Social History*, Vol. 9 (1989).

S. McKinstry, 'The Albion Motor Car Company: growth and specialisation 1899–1918', *Scottish Economic and Social History*, XI, 1991.

M. Meredith, 'Scottish Industry, *Investors Chronicle*, 22 June 1990.

A. Miller, *The rise and progress of Coatbridge* (Glasgow, 1864).

R. Miller and J. Tivy, eds., *The Glasgow Region* (Glasgow, 1958).

B.R. Mitchell, *Economic Development of the British Coal Industry 1800–1914* (Cambridge, 1984).

B.R. Mitchell and P. Deane, *Abstract of British Historical Statistics* (Cambridge, 1962).

N. Morgan, 'Disappointed Hopes', in Campbell, Duncan and Dunnett, eds., *The Story of Scotland*, No. 49, 1988.

M.S. Moss and J.R. Hume, *Workshop of the British Empire. Engineering and Shipbuilding in the West of Scotland* (London, 1977).

M. Moss and Alison Turton, *A Legend of Retailing: House of Fraser* (London, 1989).

A. Muir, *The Fife Coal Company Limited: A Short History* (Leven, 1952).

A. Muir, *Nairns of Kirkcaldy. A short history of the company 1847–1956* (Cambridge, 1956).

C.A. Oakley, *Scottish Industry To-day* (Edinburgh, 1937).

S.C. and J. Orr, 'Other Engineering', in Cunnison and Gilfillan, *Glasgow*, 1958.

P. Pagnamenta and R. Overy, *All Our Working Lives* (London, 1984).

J.R. Parkinson, 'Shipbuilding', in Buxton and Aldcroft, *British Industry*, 1979.

P.L. Payne, ed., *Studies in Scottish Business History* (London, 1967).

P.L. Payne, 'The emergence of the large-scale company in Great Britain', *Economic History Review*, Second Series, XX, 1967a.

P.L. Payne, 'Rationality and Personality: A study of mergers in the Scottish iron and steel industry, 1916–1936', *Business History*, XIX, 1977.

P.L. Payne, *Colvilles and the Scottish Steel Industry* (Oxford, 1979).

P.L. Payne, *The Early Scottish Limited Companies, 1856–1895* (Edinburgh, 1980).

P.L. Payne, 'The Decline of the Scottish Heavy Industries, 1945–1983', in Saville, ed., *Economic Development of Modern Scotland*, 1985.

P.L. Payne, *The Hydro* (Aberdeen, 1988).

Hugh B. Peebles, *Warship building on the Clyde: Naval Orders and the Prosperity of the Clyde Shipbuilding Industry, 1889–1939* (Edinburgh, 1987).

H.B. Peebles, 'A study in failure: J. & G. Thomson and Shipbuilding on Clydebank, 1871–1890', *Scottish Historical Review*, LXIX (1990).

W. Pike, 'The Construction and Installation of Offshore Petroleum Structures: The Scottish Experience' (Aberdeen, mimeo, 1990).

D. Pollock, *The Shipbuilding Industry* (London, 1905).

S. Pollard and P. Robertson, *The British Shipbuilding Industry, 1870–1914* (Cambridge, Mass., 1979).

J.N. Randall, 'New Towns and New Industries', in Saville, ed., *Economic Development of Modern Scotland*, 1985.

A. Reid, 'The Division of Labour in the British Shipbuilding Industry 1880–1920, with special reference to Clydeside'. Unpublished Ph.D. thesis, University of Cambridge, 1980.

W.G. Rimmer, *Marshall's of Leeds, Flax Spinners, 1788–1886* (Cambridge, 1960).

A.J. Robertson, 'The decline of Scottish cotton industry 1860–1914', *Business History*, XII, 1970.

P.L. Robertson, 'Shipping and shipbuilding: The Case of William Denny & Brothers', *Business History*, XVI, 1974.

A.M. Robb, 'Shipbuilding and Marine Engineering', in Cunnison and Gilfillan, *Glasgow*, 1958.

M.B. Rose, ed., *International Competition and Strategic Response in the Textile Industry since 1870* (London, 1991).

S.B. Saul, 'The Motor Industry in Britain to 1914', *Business History*, V, 1962.

R. Saville, ed., *The Economic Development of Modern Scotland, 1950–1980* (Edinburgh, 1985).

John Scott and Michael Hughes, *The Anatomy of Scottish Capital* (London, 1980).

W.R. Scott and J. Cunnison, *The Industries of the Clyde Valley during the War* (Oxford, 1924).

David Sims and M. Wood, *Car Manufacturing at Linwood: The Regional Policy Issues* (Paisley, 1984).

J. Singleton, *Lancashire on the Scrapheap. The Cotton Industry, 1945–1970* (Oxford, 1991).

A. Slaven, 'Earnings and productivity in the Scottish coal-mining industry during the nineteenth century: the Dixon enterprises', in Payne, ed., *Scottish Business History*, 1967.

A. Slaven, *The Development of the West of Scotland, 1750–1960* (London, 1975).

A. Slaven, ' "A Shipyard in Depression" John Browns of Clydebank 1919–1938', *Business History*, XIX (1977).

A. Slaven, 'Growth and Stagnation in British/Scottish Shipbuilding, 1913–1977', in Kuuse and Slaven, *Scottish and Scandinavian Shipbuilding*, 1980.

A. Slaven, 'Shipbuilding', in Daiches, ed., *Companion to Scottish Culture*, 1981.

A. Slaven, 'Self-Liquidation: the National Shipbuilders Security Ltd. and British Shipbuilding in the 1930s', in S. Palmer and G. Williams, eds., *Charted and Uncharted Waters* (London, 1981a).

A. Slaven, 'British shipbuilders: market trends and order book patterns between the wars', *Journal of Transport History*, Third Series, III (1982).

A.F. Stoddard & Co. Ltd., *The Carpet Makers* (Johnstone, 1962).

B. Supple, ed., *Essays in British Business History* (Oxford, 1977).

B. Supple, *The History of the British Coal Industry*. Vol. 4: *1913–1946: The Political Economy of Decline* (Oxford, 1987).

N.E.A. Tarrant, 'The Turkey Red Dyeing Industry in the Vale of Leven', in Butt and Ponting, *Scottish Textile History*, 1987.

A.J. Taylor, 'Labour productivity and technological innovation in the British coal industry 1830–1914', *Economic History Review*, Second Series, XIV, 1961.

S. Tolliday, *Business, Banking, and Politics: The case of British Steel, 1918–1939* (Cambridge, Mass., 1987).

G. Turnbull, *A History of the Calico Printing Industry of Great Britain* (Altrincham, 1951).

G. Turner, *Business in Britain* (London, 1969).

W. Vamplew, 'The railways and the iron industry: a study of their relationship in Scotland', in M.C. Read, ed., *Railways in the Victorian Economy*, Newton Abbot, 1969.

K. Warren, 'Locational Problems of the Scottish Iron and Steel Industry', *Scottish Geographical Magazine*, LXXXI, 1965.

K. Warren, 'Coastal Steelworks: A case for argument', *Three Banks Review*, No. 83, June, 1969.

K. Warren, 'Iron and Steel', in Buxton and Aldcroft, *British Industry*, 1979.

F.A. Wells, *Hollins and Viyella. A Study in Business History* (Newton Abbot, 1968).

F.H. Young, *A century of carpet making, 1839–1939: James Templeton & Co.* (Glasgow, n.d. [1944]).